Susie Sewell has spent a lifetime loving horses and writing about them, having a longstanding ambition to write a book. Having taught for 20 years and brought up two children, she spent a lot of time encouraging her youngest daughter's interest in dressage, when she was not looking after her eldest daughter's little boy; at this time, she was working to help students write good English and her love of language is reflected in her style of writing. Every day she would go to college with tales about a horse she had bought, a horse which actually fulfilled a lifetime's ambition to own her own dressage horse. She had taught riding, worked in stables, borrowed horses, schooled horses, but never had her own. The tales she told were greeted with such enthusiasm by her friends that it gave her the idea to write a book and share the dramatic events that befell Alira Compliquer.

To my husband, who has supported all my endeavours; and to my two daughters, who are so precious to me.

Susie Sewell

ALIRA COMPLIQUER

The True Story of Two Women and Their Horse

AUSTIN MACAULEY PUBLISHERS™

LONDON · CAMBRIDGE · NEW YORK · SHARJAH

A CIP catalogue record for this title is available from the British Library.

ISBN 9781528925709 (Paperback)
ISBN 9781528964401 (ePub e-book)

www.austinmacauley.com

First Published (2019)
Austin Macauley Publishers Ltd
25 Canada Square
Canary Wharf
London
E14 5LQ

To the people who have been kind and interested because they appreciated the beauty of my horse and to all the professionals who helped care for her.

Table of Contents

Part 1

Chapter 1
New Beginnings

The grey mare shied dramatically across the road as the pheasant clattered out of the hedgerow and glided away, oblivious to Lucy's frustration with the erratic but beautiful young horse she was riding. Now the mare was trotting forwards, ears pricked, alert as she danced sideways again, spooked by a drain rushing with water from recent rain, then on she went, her great dark eyes searching the way ahead for hazards.

Traffic was not too big a problem in this remote and scenic area of Northern Britain which Lucy was traversing via one of the many lanes and tracks through green fields, farmlands that raised cattle, sheep and horses. Pheasants were abundant because she was riding through an estate where they were bred to be shot and then grace a table at some local pub or accompany the duck and beef at a stately home nearby. But now it is a partridge that triggers another violent shy, pain shot across Lucy's back and she clenched her teeth, for this pain happens every time and is becoming almost intolerable.

A few weeks later, Lucy, Sophie and Ingrid are in the front room of their bungalow home, on a small farm which belongs to Lucy's father. The radio was on, but the mood was unusually sober, a house that was normally full of chatter and activity is somehow sombre, even the fire burns low in the grate. Forever after, Lucy and her daughters called it The Crying Song, for there was the grey mare being ridden out of the yard, her delicate half Arab, half Connemara head held high, but someone else on her back. The radio played a sad song about love and loss; Lucy choked back the tears that she thought would never stop flowing.

All her life she had wanted a horse, but always ridden for others, never owned and held onto one. Now this beautiful little horse was going too, never to dance along the lanes with her, gallop over the fields with her, never again to jump the boughs and becks and troughs they had jumped or grace the field outside the house.

They all cried and hugged each other. Lucy made tea and they continued to pack, for they were moving house that day too. She thought her heart would break, because it was probably the end of her riding career. Too many changes afoot, too little money, too much pain, physical and emotional; too many hours on the chiropractor's couch, neck bones crunched, back clicked, days after riding when she could not straighten up, could not bend down.

The love of horses, the freedom to ride, had sustained Lucy through a turbulent, restless life, where she could not settle. Now, it may not be possible to ride anymore, she was leaving behind the option of keeping a horse and they were facing an uncertain future, burning their bridges; the family was setting out alone.

Ingrid, the younger of the two girls, felt the departure of the mare and leaving the farm most keenly. She felt for her mother, seeing her tears, knowing about the pain which her mother hid from her family much of the time. Ingrid knew that fear of her grandfather's anger kept her mum working hard out on the farm to pay the rent and keep their little house. Indeed, as soon as her dad was home from work, he would be out there too and Ingrid and Sophie would amuse themselves or work as well.

She, like her mum, loved the animals, the feel of thick sheep's wool between her fingers, the smell of new-mown hay, the soft eyes and big ears of the cattle. Lucy had tried to impart her love of horses to both her daughters, Ingrid, who was 10 years old and Sophie, who was 16. Both had ridden since they were small. Lucy had gone on too long working on the farm, hard physical work which tore damaged muscles and pushed her past her limits. So, Lucy and James left the farm and the little house, to rely on their own jobs to try and set up home far away.

Chapter 2
Dreams Do Come True

Fast forwards fifteen years. An older Lucy stands in an indoor school, watching a powerful little Warmblood mare being carefully schooled by a slender, elegant young woman who sits motionless in the saddle, guiding the fiery horse by imperceptible aids from her legs and sensitive hands on the reins. She and her horse are in harmony; Lucy admires the fluent canter, the dynamic trot, the crossing of forelegs and hind legs as the mare yields to the left and then to the right, an accomplished rider in the saddle.

Why would her daughter not be gifted in the equestrian art? Ingrid had to have inherited some gift, some gene that had kept all the ancestors of this woman fascinated by horses, bound to them down the generations. Lucy calls Ingrid to her side and smiles as the sweating horse comes to a gradual halt beside her, then stands obediently, chewing her bit and slightly tossing her expressive head, her bay neck arched, her forelegs and hind legs placed square, her muscled body held in readiness for the next command.

She is the dream. She is the epitome of all the frustrated desires of three generations of horse lovers and the culmination of an amazing journey; she carries the standard which is a tribute to determination, belief and love. Ingrid rides a horse which when they left the farm was an impossible dream for her and her mother and now is a successful dressage horse, but to get here there have been many, many trials and barriers to cross.

Lucy cannot ride anymore, it is too late for her, but she enjoys this horse and Ingrid's success vicariously, as coach, groom, assistant and confidante. This book is the story of the journey, the ecstasy and the agony that is part of owning such a very special horse.

Time had passed since they left the farm and hard work of a different kind had enabled Lucy and James to successfully keep a home and educate their children. Lucy's husband left the army and trained to teach driving and Lucy herself had utilised a hard-won Open University degree to teach in Further Education. Sophie was working in London and Ingrid had become a psychologist, so was earning her own income. The day had come where Lucy and Ingrid decided they could perhaps afford to have a horse, if they pooled their resources and shared the expenses. They searched for two years! Were told lies, deceived, drawn far afield to no avail and disappointed time after time. Horses were smaller than advertised, not sound, overpriced and some downright dangerous!

Chapter 3
Finding 'The One'

Finally, Ingrid saw a short film on the internet of a bay mare under saddle with a tall man on her back, who wanted to sell her because he was six feet three inches tall and the mare only 15.2 hands high. He had just backed her so she was ready to school on.

Lucy looked at the clip on the internet and liked her. "Where is she?" she asked.

When Ingrid replied, "Sussex," Lucy laughed.

"But we live in the North! That's quite a journey."

But after going to see yet another horse, advertised as fit whose legs looked as if he had trousers on, Ingrid relented and off they went to see yet another possibility. They had to wait until they could get time off work then decided to make a weekend of it. Speeding down the M25 in Ingrid's Fiat Punto, they thought they had not much further to go; it was Spring Bank Holiday weekend and they had decided to stay over in Aldershot, for old times' sake – Lucy and James had lived there when they were first married and he was still in the Army. Their aim was to see the horse first thing in the morning.

"Something is wrong!" shrieked Ingrid, helplessly turning the steering wheel as a sinister grinding sound began to be emitted from the engine.

Lucy grabbed the wheel yelling, "Foot off the gas!" and they slowly coasted onto the hard shoulder of the motorway, hazard lights on, coming eventually to an abrupt halt, horns blasting around them.

Efforts to start the car again were futile, so they got out and climbed behind the crash barrier, ringing the breakdown service quickly, wondering how long they would have to wait; it *would* have to be a Bank Holiday weekend!

Two tall blonde ladies at the side of the motorway caused some distraction. Lucy was in hysterics as waggon drivers catcalled and blasted their horns.

"But we're mother and daughter," she laughed, "don't they realise!"

Ingrid was faintly offended and snorted in derision, "They should focus on the road!"

When the breakdown company finally came, their verdict on the car was dire. They would recover it to the nearest garage but there was no way they could go any further in it, nor was it going to be mended this weekend. Alternatively, they could recover it to a garage near home.

"Come on," said Lucy, "Let's give up on this horse, it's not meant to be. We have to think of the cost implications. Let's go home."

But Ingrid was adamant. "They'll take us to Aldershot and then we'll hire a car to get to Sussex tomorrow!"

Some argument ensued about the possibility of getting hold of another car, phone calls were attempted but they had no signal. The day was wearing on and the dust and noise were incessant. Ingrid seemed strangely insistent on seeing this horse, but Lucy was more cautious; it might be a waste of time, like all the others. Not be as good as it looked, not be what they said, and what about the price?

Ultimately, they piled into the low loader that was now carrying the car and were dropped off where they were staying by the kindly woman who was driving for the rescue company.

"You're lucky!" She exclaimed. "We're not really supposed to do this, but you are my last call out and I live in Aldershot."

Gratefully, they dragged their bags out of the high vehicle and stumbled to their room.

Lots of anxious phoning that evening resulted in two Gurkha men arriving with a hire car the following morning, which Ingrid had paid for on her credit card.

"Can both of us drive the car?" Lucy asked.

"Well, Madam, it's like this, you see, you drive the car. You see policeman, you move over seat and you say she drive the car. No problem!"

"Okay," said Lucy, while Ingrid dissolved into a fit of giggles.

They were in high spirits as they left for Sussex, Ingrid driving, Lucy orienteering.

Driving through green fields in the sunshine, Lucy saw a flash of movement and spotted a Peregrine Falcon dive like an arrow from the sky to capture another bird, quickly out of sight among the trees. She was thrilled, having loved birds all her life, but had never seen a Peregrine Falcon and to see it kill was awesome, the speed and precision of it, to think that such a small bird can dive at nearly 200 miles an hour.

Lucy thought this must be highly significant but was immediately distracted by Ingrid asking, "Which way at this junction?"

They stopped and studied the map to no avail, ultimately deciding to ring the owner of the horse for the final directions. He was the epitome of kindness and said it was a bit tricky so he would drive out to meet them and they could follow him to his stables. Soon they were careering after him as he sped through cornfields and consequently to a big wooden gate. They followed him into the yard and came to a halt in tranquil surroundings; old barns, high spreading trees and well swept pathways.

"I have got her in out of the field," said Lenny, after he had introduced himself. "Come this way."

He was a handsome, well-spoken individual who they knew was a professional dressage rider but told them he was also breeding horses on a small scale here. They followed him into a big stable yard where many horses' heads looked over the doors of loose boxes and so to one with the bay mare inside.

Lenny led her out and she stood patiently for them to admire her, but each woman was cautious not to seem too enthusiastic – he'd only put the price up! Ingrid and Lucy both thought she was lovely though! Her bay coat gleamed in the sun and her proportions were ideal; Lucy remembered the pictures of good conformation in horse books she had read and this little mare matched them all!

Feeling carefully over the warm sleek body, there was nothing of concern, only a bony protrusion on the coronet of her off foreleg, which Lenny explained was due to being stepped on as a youngster. An almost imperceptible line across her chest was another accident which had occurred as a young horse. She had galloped into a fence, he said.

"What is her name?" asked Ingrid, to be told it was Alira.

Lucy gasped, "Wow! A name full of promise!"

Lenny looked perplexed and Lucy quickly tried to explain that she thought it was a lovely name, but that names can infer a lot and it was so unusual that it could mean many things. Lenny looked at her as if she was crazy and proceeded to put some tack on Alira whilst Lucy held her.

"Well, we just chose that because it is traditional to call a filly a name starting with the same letter as her mother and her dam was called Attitude."

Ingrid suppressed a wry smile at this, in view of what her mum had just said and that in horses there is often a genetic link between the character of a filly and her dam.

The mare was barely four years old now and Lenny stated that she was quiet and good to ride; so next, the trio of people led her into an outdoor arena surrounded by neat fencing of wooden boards, with a long mirror at the top.

"Nobody else has ridden her except for me, so I am not sure what she will think of you getting on," he said to Ingrid.

Ingrid's face paled, for much as she was an experienced rider, she had not ridden much for the last five years whilst getting her degree, then starting her first job. But this horse was for her and she could not consider it without having ridden her!

Carefully, she lowered herself into the saddle – and felt little resistance. Walked her round the big, spacious arena, felt a push into trot that reflected this mare's marvellous stride; she felt like a much bigger horse and conveyed a feeling of power and fluency. Ingrid gently put her legs on to ask for canter and off she went, too fast because she was inexperienced and unbalanced, but lively, rhythmical, exciting.

Ingrid thought, *I should slow or stop now*, but she seemed to have no brakes and carried on round.

She was laughing now, laughing with the sheer joy of it, the unbridled, bouncy, exhilarating joy of it! When she did manage to stop at last, her face was flushed and beaming. Careful not to be too enthusiastic, she walked the horse around to calm her and found that she could get her to bend and turn. She was obedient to the rein and sort of understood leg aids, although not very well, but for her this was a new rider, talking a different language, making different demands and the mare was hesitant.

Lucy and Ingrid had agreed not to discuss their response in front of Lenny, for Lucy already felt that he might think these women were very keen, to have come so far and arrived so promptly. Another look over her and Lucy announced that they would go and have some lunch and consider their views, then, if it was acceptable to Lenny, pop back. He directed them to a small village nearby where there was a decent café and away they went, leaving behind the gracious affluence of the stable yard and surroundings, driving down between the big fields, along a narrow lane and so to the café.

After they had sat down and ordered scrambled eggs they looked at each other in silence; a slow smile spread across Ingrid's stunning face and Lucy's serious grey eyes looked tearful.

She was the first to speak. "I think we've found her!"

"Oh yes, she's brilliant, so much the best so far!" Ingrid was exultant.

Two long years of searching and this animal seemed to have so much of what they wanted, including the conformation, the right size, a mare so there was the capacity to breed from her if their plans changed or she was not sound at some point; she seemed to have the character and the looks. True, she was only four, which was younger than ideal; they both had been around horses a lot, but had not had extensive experience, had not brought on a youngster from only just being backed.

However, the realisation was dawning that the ideal horse which was trained to do dressage already – for that was what Ingrid wanted to do – was unaffordable. Now as they finished their lunch, Lucy was trying to be the responsible parent and pointed out that they could not actually afford what Lenny was asking and their hopes lay in being able to bargain him down.

"We've got to be prepared to walk away," she said now, "that is, if we expect to get him to lower his price."

"Yes but… what if he sells her to somebody else?" Ingrid was aghast.

"That's a risk we'll have to take," said Lucy firmly, although she really did not want to take that risk at all!

Lucy put her lipstick back on and Ingrid retied her blonde ponytail. When they arrived back at the stables, Lenny was pleased to see them. They had another look at Alira in her stable;

she was standing calmly munching on some hay. Lenny suggested they come to his accommodation, which was a flat within the stately and huge farmhouse that graced the top side of the stable yard. He gestured towards a well-worn and comfortable-looking settee and asked if they would like coffee or tea.

Whilst he made it, he indicated a large deep freeze and said, "I have just put some more semen in there," at which Lucy and Ingrid sat bolt upright with shock.

What on earth was he talking about? "I import it from the best stallions that are standing at stud in Germany; it would be far too costly to send my mares over there."

Now they understood. They relaxed a little, but all too soon broached the question of money. Lucy made an offer they could afford and he was not accepting it, so she pointed out that the mare was young and untried, had some scars on her, could not jump and most people buying a horse want it to be able to jump.

He hesitated, then said, "But I am only interested in dressage, dressage is what this yard is all about, breaking in and breeding dressage horses."

They tried to argue and he started to waver, dropped his price a little but not enough. Eventually, he said he would sleep on it. If they came back tomorrow he would consider their offer but hoped they would come halfway to meet him. They said they would not, but would come back tomorrow, very much hoping he would accept their offer, because they were going back up North tomorrow, had no more time.

Off they went back to Aldershot, discussing the mare, discussing Lenny, making exciting plans, but not daring to plan too much. After all, she was not theirs yet! They spent the evening trying to locate the Army flats which James and Lucy had lived in when they were first married, only to find they had been pulled down and a new, featureless estate had been built instead. Lucy felt gloomy and wondered if it was another omen; she was an intelligent woman, but so passionate about horses that she was prepared to be far less logical where they were concerned!

The following morning, they were at the stables in good early time, for they had the long journey home to make in a hire car which was not a vehicle they were used to driving, it was okay, but not inspiring. There was no sign of Lenny, so they loitered outside the big wooden gate, not wanting to intrude.

After ten minutes or so, they spotted two riders coming down the lane and as they came closer realised one was Lenny, on a tall black horse and he was accompanied by a woman on another, fiery looking, heavier bay horse.

When the two riders got to the gate, they dismounted and Lenny introduced the owner of the premises, who was tall, gaunt and frightfully upper class. They put their horses away and the woman vanished into the big house. Lenny made casual chat – he seemed to like them and Ingrid in particular! Lucy was hopeful.

"Anyway, about buying this horse. Will you accept our offer?"

Lenny sat down on a bench near the stable where Alira stood in the shade, away from the hot sun. "Well…" he said slowly, "I'd be really disappointed in myself if I did. You see, I reared her and I think she is special, I would keep her to train myself if she had been 16.2 hands high like she was supposed to be."

"Absolutely!" Lucy jumped at her chance; "Nobody will pay more for her, people want a bigger horse for dressage! You have to think too, you have met us and like us and I can promise you we will give her a brilliant home, she'll never want for anything, we won't overwork her, she will be our only horse and the two of us will cherish her."

Lenny was wavering. Ingrid brought home their advantage, saying, "You can come and see her any time you want to, we will not mind, you can check she is okay and see how she is progressing!"

"Oh, I could," replied Lenny. "My girlfriend lives up North." (*Oh no*, thought Ingrid, *he's got a girlfriend*).

Lucy felt triumphant; they had nearly got their little horse!

"We could pay cash as well," she said.

Lenny was just about to reply when the lady from the big house reappeared. "I am just about to accept their offer for Alira," he told her and the elegant woman turned towards Lucy and Ingrid.

"No, he's not. He will not let her go for a penny less than the asking price. He would be foolish if he did," and she scowled at Lenny.

Lucy and Ingrid were furious. Why did she have to intervene? What was it to her anyway? Why didn't she just go away? Sure enough, she had hardened Lenny's resolve and he then stuck to his original price.

"Well, we will have to leave it then, we need to go now," said Lucy with genuine sadness and Lenny walked them back to where their car was in the gateway.

"Are you sure you will not change your mind?" begged Lucy.

Lenny looked genuinely disappointed but that woman clearly had some kind of hold over him and now he would not budge.

They got in the car, disconsolate and unable to believe that they were leaving the answer to their dreams behind. Lucy lowered the window.

"I will ring you this afternoon just in case you change your mind."

The interfering woman was out of earshot and he grinned but said, "I don't think I will."

They drove away expostulating.

"If she hadn't come he was going to agree!" this came from Ingrid and Lucy spat a reply, "That is so unfair! We have wasted our journey now and I feel so disappointed."

Ingrid agreed, "She is the perfect horse for us, but he's never going to change his mind again now."

They drove on in silence, a cloud of gloom in the car. Hours passed as they battled with the M25 and then journeyed on, long shards of motorway disappearing under their wheels, taking them further away from their dream horse, the one they wanted so much.

Many hours later, they drove into a service station and ordered coffee for Ingrid, tea for Lucy.

"Shall I ring?"

"May as well, but it might not be worth bothering."

A few minutes later, the hundreds of people in the busy service station all stopped to look as an ear-piercing shriek rent the air and two women leapt up from their chairs, hugging and crying. He had accepted their offer – the little bay mare was going to be theirs!

Chapter 4
Getting Their Impossible Dream

Lucy had never imagined being able to afford a horse. Ingrid had never imagined such a perfect horse. A gruff old man had spoken to them, amused at their delight, "Have you bought a horse then? Well, that's the cheapest thing you'll ever do, you know?"

That man was so right. The outlay initially is a tiny proportion of what a horse costs to keep. Just then, Lucy and Ingrid did not want to hear that, they were just starting out on their journey as horse owners!

When they got home, Lucy started to organise bringing the mare up from the South. She rang a well-known horse transport firm, for they had no trailer or horsebox. She was quoted a big price, told that their precious horse would share the huge horsebox with eighteen others and she would have to go all over the countryside while the box was collecting more horses before she finally got home.

That did not seem very good, so Lucy and James took a trip out to a farm that advertised the use of a small horsebox. This was successful; the vehicle looked well maintained and they were nice people, their farm a menagerie with hens of all sizes, dogs, goats and of course, horses.

The guy was friendly and told stories of his past as a military man, then they found themselves by a field fence where his wife kept her two large horses. The horses leaned over to him in his wheelchair, breathing meadow-scented breath and then returning to munch the hay nets strung on the fence.

"This is peace," he said and the three of them felt that relaxation of just being near big animals that are calm and accepting, that have no designs on a lovely spring evening other than to munch through their quota of hay. James looked at his lovely wife and he knew that if horses were what it took to make her happy, then he wanted a horse as much as she did.

Lucy made arrangements to collect the box the following day and they set off home excited and happy. It was a small horsebox, so any of them could drive it, but James had extensive experience driving big machines as well as a licence for heavy goods vehicles.

"What are you grinning about?" asked James on the way home, glancing at Lucy's imperfect profile (the consequence of a riding accident) and seeing a smile on her lips.

"It's great, it's all happening," she replied and James said, "Don't get too excited, you know you do daft things when you are on a roll."

Lucy laughed good-naturedly and assured him that she would not, this was for Ingrid as well as her and everything had to go right.

The day dawned bright and breezy; they made an early start to beat the traffic and to cover the long distance ahead of them. Even a small horsebox such as they were using affords an admirable view in comparison to a car, so James drove and Lucy and Inga sat squeezed in next to him, chatting happily and making plans. They had booked a livery stable at an establishment run for the advantage of Military personnel, able to be given a place by virtue of James working for the Ministry of Defence. They had ordered some rubber matting for the stable because it did look rather an uneven floor that should be arriving today.

They hummed along the motorway, it seemed as if nothing could possibly go wrong; true, it was daunting to have the responsibility for a horse, from today, but she was sure they could manage. There was just a nagging worry in Lucy's mind about the conflict of both of them having a full-time job and the consequent limitations of being otherwise engaged from nine to five, but they would work around that. Neither of them had ever been afraid of hard work and horses had to deal with those hours in between; they just went out in the field.

They drew up at Lenny's place as a fierce sun was starting to drop out of the sky, silhouetting the tall trees behind the stable yard. Lenny was waiting for them and That Woman was lurking, the one who had stopped him from accepting Lucy's initial offer.

Alira was in the stable and immediately disgraced herself by kicking at James when he went to put bandages on to protect her legs, but then accepted the head collar that Ingrid put over her head. One thing they did not check was whether she had ever travelled before and now they learned that no, she had not been transported anywhere since she was a foal. Ingrid cringed a little, she felt they looked like amateurs as Lucy produced the woolly stable bandages to protect her legs in the horsebox, they had no travel boots, no kit like that at this stage!

Suddenly, events were taken out of their hands, as the pompous lady and Lenny went into overdrive, fastened a contraption around Alira's head with a big metal hoop outstanding above her ears (could it be they thought she might rear?). The woman led her firmly and quickly towards the horsebox ramp and bundled her into the box, Lenny embracing her quarters from behind in a sort of rugby tackle that left the mare with little choice other than to go forwards. The partition was shut and Lucy popped into the back to tie her up, realising that poor Alira was starting to panic somewhat. Their precious cargo was loaded.

"She seems a bit agitated," Lucy said anxiously. "What shall we do if she doesn't calm down?" this as resounding kicks and bangs could be heard from the waggon.

"Just keep driving," said Lenny, "she'll get used to it."

They shook hands and the imperious woman commented, "Yes, I think you will have a lot of fun with that little horse."

These words would echo down the years in their ambiguity. Did she say this with sincerity or sarcastic irony? Was it a suggestion of a future full of joy with Alira or an ominous indication of what her previous owners actually knew about her?

"She'll be okay once you get going," repeated Lenny.

At this, James climbed into the driving seat, Ingrid got into the middle and finally Lucy jumped in and slammed the door. They set off on an enthralling journey, but motion seemed to do nothing to calm the mare and as they drove through the small village where Lucy and Inga had first decided they wanted to buy her, the kicking reached a crescendo and then such banging and clattering!

"She's down! Stop!" Lucy's face was ashen. They had hardly started the journey and it sounded like the horse was upside down in her stall sustaining who knew what injuries, disaster had happened so soon! James pulled over and the two women jumped out and opened the back door, to be greeted very vocally by an upstanding horse, almost engulfed in a cloud of steam, nostrils flared, lathered with sweat, apparently cantering on the spot.

"Whoa, whoa, you are okay, steady, girl," – comforted by their presence the mare started to snatch at the hay they had provided her with, but her muscles were bunched and tense and if they turned to leave, she dropped the hay from her mouth, whinnied and shrieked, rearing in an attempt to escape her stall.

Lucy took hold of her head collar only to have her hand smacked against the metal upright of the stall.

"I think we will just have to keep driving like Lenny said."

They opened some windows to cool her down and got back in the cab. Driving onwards, the back of Lucy's hand became a hematoma, like a small purple volcano erupting unbidden on the back of her hand. The first of many war wounds!

The long journey continued, mostly driven by James while Lucy sat feeling as if her stomach was in a knot, agonising over whether their new charge was going to survive this journey unscathed, flinching every time an unshod hoof whacked the side of the horsebox. The spring day was beginning to fade as they drove northwards, the sun now dropping behind the familiar horizon of the Pennine Hills.

Ingrid, as ever, was thinking and planning, "We'll have to get her shod behind to protect those small back feet."

It was the only thing that the vetting had raised as an issue, that her hind hooves were quite small. A minor consideration they thought, they did not look very different to any other horse's hooves. Apart from this, her confirmation was almost perfect and not many horses have that gift.

They had arranged a stable at a small livery yard about three or four miles from their home and when they arrived the yard was quiet. Most people had done evening stables and they could park in the yard near to the loose box which was booked for her. The ramp came down and there she was! All in one piece, head high, ears pricked, eyes staring at this new place. A stunning horse stood at the top of the ramp and she was theirs!

Soon, the animal was installed in the stable, fed and watered and seemed happy to eat hay, but what took them by surprise was the size and solidity of the mare; yes, she was only 15.2 hands high but she could only just turn around in this stable, so it did not seem too comfortable for her.

The following morning, another problem was apparent: the place was full of little black flies! Adjacent to the muckheap, with the sun shining straight in, poor Alira was agitated as they tickled her thin, sensitive skin. Ingrid did morning stables before she went to work, the first of many five o'clock starts – the pattern of her life as a horse owner. Both she and Lucy worked full time, but that day Lucy managed to get an early finish and drove directly to the stables.

Chapter 5
What Had They Bought?

Delighted to see the lovely little horse, Lucy made a fuss of her, stroking her shiny neck, patting her big, firm shoulder, checking over the rest of her – brown, black mane and tail, three little socks, a tiny star, more of an asterisk really. Slipping on the head collar, Lucy took her out for a walk, not expecting any problems whatsoever. But the minute they were out of the yard, Alira became some demon horse from hell. She was up in the air, she was round in a circle, snorting, strong as an ox, wild as an untrained mustang; wow, she looked beautiful, but boy was she strong.

Lucy held her through sheer determination, struggled through a field gate just to have some safety that if she did get away she couldn't get onto the road. This seemed to make Alira wilder and more determined to bolt. Lucy was feeling more exhausted by the minute.

What have we bought? she thought, as the big bay mare seemed to gain another hand or two, her head so high and her action so elevated, her eye was wild and she just seemed crazy. She barged into Lucy repeatedly and when Lucy tightened her grip on her, she came around at speed and spun her in a circle, only then to half rear and bound forwards in a bid to be gone.

Lucy was amazed at this extreme behaviour and had one thought in her mind: to get her back into the stable before she escaped and killed herself in some mad dash for freedom, or broke a leg bolting from some monster only she could see. Soothing words had no effect on her; she was showing the whites of her eyes, fixated with fear.

Somehow, Lucy battled her back to the stable, got her breath back only to think again, *What on earth have we bought?*

Later that same evening, Inga and Lucy together put a bridle on with a rein at either side and set off towards the indoor school. Alira was crazy again but could not be quite so wild with somebody at either side, both equally determined to calm and settle her, definitely adamant that they weren't going to lose her.

Upon reaching the confines of the indoor school, Alira seemed able to listen to them and was prepared to be lunged, which gave her exercise and instilled some obedience. They had no saddle for her yet. Ingrid had been keen to ride bareback at first, until they got a saddle, she was an accomplished rider; but the mare's behaviour had made her think twice!

The following day, Ingrid did ride bareback, with Lucy alongside. Now Ingrid really felt the power of her stride! It was like a great push, up through Ingrid's back and towards her horse's ears; no other horse had ever felt like this! Trotting was out of the question, it was unlikely she would be able to stay seated. But there was a thrill to this horse, a *forwardness*, that just made her want to ride her again – get a saddle and find out what all her paces were like.

The next few days passed like lightening, each of them going to work as well as making time to go the stables, trying to give their new horse some form of routine, do all the feeding, mucking out, grooming and so on, but leave time to see partners, eat and sleep! Alongside this, they managed to arrange a saddle fitting, having quickly discovered that no standard saddle was wide enough for her broad and muscular back. Ultimately, they found an air-filled saddle which accommodated her high withers as well.

With trepidation, Inga rode her into the arena, but Alira walked, trotted and even cantered without any objection, although once again the third pace left Inga feeling she did not have much control, as the mare's head came down heavily on the bit. The four-year-old was just unbalanced and had such an extravagantly long stride that she pushed herself onto her shoulders even more than most young horses do. Ingrid was to spend long hours trying to get her to carry herself with more weight behind and her hind legs underneath her. Just then though, it was all very thrilling and exciting and not a problem!

Chapter 6
The Outsiders

Their first livery stables turned out to be not entirely suitable for Alira, because of the small size of the loose box itself, the irritating little black flies and the field which was available for turning out the horse. Unfortunately, this latter was full of large stones, irregularly fenced and dangerously infested by ragwort. The energy of Alira was such that it was obvious she would gallop as soon as they turned her out and being so nervous, she may run into or go through one of those fences, injure herself on a stone or, being a naïve filly, eat some poisonous ragwort. None of these things were risks they were prepared to take, so within a week they had found another livery stable, an Equitation Centre this time, that had big green fields which were well fenced and the stable they had been shown looked okay, being slightly bigger and not so near a muck heap. Someone was able to come and collect Alira, who did take quite a lot of persuading to mount the steep ramp to join another two horses inside! Ingrid literally had to lift her hind hooves onto the ramp – having got that far, some coaxing with delicious food persuaded her to run up and turn to be tied.

Once Alira was installed into her new stable, the problems really began. Not with the horse this time, but with the people. There were half a dozen other women who had their horses liveried there and they had been there a long time. Their habit was to spend much of their time not looking after their horses but sitting in a small group, gossiping, drinking coffee and criticising anyone and everyone other than themselves. Because Lucy and Ingrid were always friendly, they thought a smile and a few friendly chats would overcome this, but it only seemed to harden the hatred which slowly grew against them. The malice seemed to centre around the field arrangements for Alira; initially they had asked if she could have a separate field, just until she got used to more new surroundings. The woman who ran the yard was small, smoked heavily and wore a lot of make-up, but seemed pleasant enough and had agreed.

However, the arrangement only lasted a couple of days, after which Lucy and Ingrid were told that they must put her in with 'the herd'. This was a huge gang of about twenty horses, mixed mares and geldings, who ran together in a large open field. They were assured, erroneously, that this would be the only way to get her used to other horses, so they must just get on with it. Lucy felt very dubious, but anyway, she walked round the field first, just as her father had always taught her to, to find any litter, stones, sharp objects and to check the fences.

Oh, how this made them bitch! "Who does she think she is? What is so special about her horse anyway?" were the kind of comments muttered between cigarettes, smoked in the stable barns. This latter habit appalled Lucy and that was not because she was a snob as they seemed to think – had they never read *Black Beauty*, the famous children's story about horses has a dramatic passage where some horses die in a fire….

The morning dawned bright and sunny when Lucy went to turn Alira out with the herd for the first time. Through the field gate, Lucy turned her around and released the head collar. Suddenly, Alira was surrounded by the whole herd, sniffing, squealing, snorting, jostling to see this new addition to their numbers. Alira trotted away in an elevated, graceful trot, her beautiful head held high, her mane tossed behind – the others followed, then the next minute surged forwards into a gallop and off they went! Right around the field, Alira caught up in the melee, towards the back, as they wheeled in a big circle.

Then to Lucy's horror, Alira's hind legs slipped from under her and momentarily, Lucy thought she was going to come down, but she saved herself and re-joined the herd, which slowed now and seemed to somewhat lose interest in the newcomer. One or two started grazing, but one in particular still seemed very interested in Alira; a bay gelding, wiry and not any bigger than she, but seemingly under the illusion that he was a stallion. Lucy was walking in the field to check the water trough and Alira appeared at her shoulder, anxious, muttering, looking like a large foal who has lost her mummy. The gelding was hot on her heels, weaving his neck over her, not hurting her but persistent, agitating her.

"Go on" said Lucy, "Go and join the others," but her mare seemed much more interested in what Lucy herself was doing.

Time would pass and they would realise that Alira identified with humans more than with other horses, possibly because she had been bottle-fed, but they did not know it then and their horse would pay dearly for her inability to read the signs and signals that pass between horses and allow them to read each other's intentions.

That evening, Ingrid brought Alira back into the stable and was dismayed to find the bleeding imprint of a horseshoe at one side of her tail. Carefully, it was cleaned and dressed with wound cream, but Lucy and Ingrid were not happy. *What if it scarred her or became infected?* They were not sure about this herd business and went to convey their concerns to the woman who ran the livery yard: blonde, middle-aged and heavily made up to look younger than her years, but the effect was ruined by her resemblance to a duck, with her squat body and uneven gait. The consequence of her speaking was to make Lucy want to laugh out loud, because she *sounded* like a duck, softly quacking – a consequence of years of heavy smoking. Lucy, of course, did not laugh, but tried to counteract her own tendency to feel humbled by anyone more horsey than herself by not letting go of the duck image entirely. The sharp retort about Alira being in or out of the herd was to say she would 'Just have to get used to it', delivered as she walked away on some supposedly more important business.

Alira went out again the following day, into the danger zone, came in with another kick likewise the following day. This resulted in Lucy and Ingrid going to make a specific request for a small field, which they had seen was empty, to put Alira in by herself to prevent these injuries. Even just a few hours a day would be fine. But Pamela, the duck-like proprietor, suggested another field, one they were grateful for and said so. Their mare seemed happy in this field and that day they left her with less concerns; there would be no kicks when they came back!

Returning after work, Lucy felt tranquil as she walked from the yard down the lane; there was a fresh spring breeze blowing – still cold, but in the sunshine, there was that hint of warmth that promises more to come. The blue sky was cloudless except for a fluffy white bank in the distance and Lucy had a spring in her step.

Seeing Alira, Lucy had cause again to admire the pretty head that was raised to observe her presence, when she halted in her stride. There was an enormous hole in the field! About four feet deep and the area of a small building, it must have been dug during the day while Alira was in there; tyre tracks of the digger were evident from the gateway. *Surely not!* Lucy gazed in disbelief. What if their mare had got out while they brought the digger in, or fallen in the hole, how much galloping around had she done and at what cost to her legs? But maybe somebody had come and taken her in?

When she looked in the hole, this seemed unlikely, because it was full of Alira's hoof prints! Appalled, she caught the horse and checked her over, relieved to find no apparent injury. Lucy was slightly impressed that Alira must have jumped in and out again; she had potential as a jumper perhaps. Back up in the stable yard, nobody seemed to know anything and Pamela was nonchalant and non-committal when asked about it.

Lucy was firm in her statement when she said, "Well, she can't stay in there, if there is work going on."

So now they were assigned a little paddock to share with an old, broken down pony. This field needed attention to the fences and a lot of poo picking doing, but such was their desperation that they were happy to do it all, the fencing as well; at a do-it-yourself livery-stable it really is what it says, you do it yourself! Alira actually was reassured by the staid old pony and things might have got better, but the next day they started parking the tractor in the stable next door to Alira. When the engine was revved up Alira was terrified, but once again, it happened when neither Lucy nor Ingrid were there and seemed almost designed to upset their highly temperamental horse and make her unable to settle down. Ingrid was riding her now, but finding her strong, unpredictable and volatile; none of the surroundings the young mare found herself in were likely to reduce any of her fear and nervousness. Barking dogs, a bicycle, even a shadow would make her whip round, prepared to bolt, so exercising her was certainly not relaxing!

Lots of people who saw her said, "Oh, what a beautiful horse!" Especially when she was prancing, head thrown up, ears pricked, her dark and slightly dished face monitoring her surroundings, champing her bit and lifting her feet expressively high. She certainly had the qualities of a dressage horse, but not a quiet hack! She was different in the indoor school, where it was quiet and she could be worked in a contained environment. Ingrid loved these times, when she could concentrate on riding her well and developing both her and her horse's considerable potential.

"There must be an element of jealousy. Why do they dislike us so much?" proclaimed Ingrid, who had just finished evening stables to the tune of their laughter and chat, which stopped immediately when she walked past.

Lucy experienced the same, frosty silence greeting her cheery 'Good morning' as she passed them on the way to the muck heap. The older of the two women suddenly looked tired and unhappy; she disliked any bad feeling. "Yes, I reckon they are jealous that we have a horse like her, but they will just have to get over it." Inwardly, Ingrid felt furious, but she did not want to make a scene, so carried on, saying nothing.

Lucy had hung up her riding boots after the grey mare was taken away from the farm, finding herself incapacitated by pain when she got out of bed in the morning, getting moving by stages, but still suffering acutely when she lifted too much, unable to tolerate even the impact of riding her bike, finding the chronic nature of the pain in her back and neck wore her down. Repetitive movement caused as much pain as no movement, which resulted in spasm and stiffness. Consequently, her enjoyment of the horse was to be vicarious. She would be Ingrid's coach and groom, facilitating her pursuit of a dressage career. Ingrid had already had some success with this on a riding school horse and she loved the precision, the focus of schooling a horse to improve its movement and way of going, its ability to do its job in any capacity.

Alira was too green to ride her on the busy roads surrounding the Equestrian Centre, so Lucy would lead her out to educate her. She reassured her about vehicles, holding her in at the side of the road, gesturing to them to slow down and making a big fuss of the mare if she stood still, albeit that she was trembling and very alert. The first time a bicycle whizzed into view, Alira whipped round as fast as lightning and tried to bolt for home, how Lucy hung on she never knew. Alira was only in a head collar and it was sheer desperation not to let her go on the road that kept Lucy on the end of the rope, her legs flying to keep up with her body as she ran with her, ultimately pulling her round and to a halt. The horse was wired now as Lucy took her back past the bike and the cars that had appeared. Alira felt as if she had grown to 17.2 instead of 15.2 hands high. She was snorting with fear, still pumped by the adrenaline shooting through her veins. Lucy silently thanked God that she hadn't let her go, hardly daring to imagine the consequences of a mile-long gallop back to the stable, the sharp turn into the lane that would surely have brought her down.

But life with Alira was never complicated by just one problem, they always escalated from one to another. Now, as she was leading the anxious horse along the road to take her back to the sanctity of the stables, vehicle after vehicle was suddenly passing them; huge waggons came squeezing past in the narrow lane, revving their engines and grinding their gears, followed by rattling tractors towing trailers and impatient commuters hurrying home from work. Unknown to Lucy, a closure on the A1 motorway had diverted all this traffic down a country road and turned her enjoyable walk into a nightmare.

Lucy's arms ached from holding the strong little horse, who was attracting much admiration with her head held high, her prancing hooves and muscular body compacted for 'fight or flight'. Lucy vowed she would have a bridle on her next time, but no use now to do other than talk to her, elbow her in the shoulder to hold her back as she curved her neck to allow for the propulsion of her body. Even when they finally turned off the road, the lane up to the stables had never seemed so long and Alira was still full of excitement and feeling just as strong and just as keen to bolt.

Next time Lucy walked her out, she decided to go across the fields, down a path that ran adjacent to the indoor arena, with Alira wearing her bridle this time, so that the bit in her mouth gave her a little more control. All went well initially, Alira was being sweet and calm, Lucy's steps synchronising with the mare's long, loose and easy walk; onwards they went, past cornfields and grass meadows, enjoying the absence of traffic and the rural scenery around them. They were passing a small cottage when suddenly, frenzied barking erupted from behind a wire gate, as three dogs hurled themselves against it, barking furiously at these unaccustomed intruders. Alira reacted with a violent shy which lifted Lucy clean off her feet and propelled her not only across the path but the wide verge beside it – somehow she landed on her feet, kept upright by the big brown body of her horse – and once again had to fight the mare' s urge to bolt. Some distance had to be gained between her and the dogs before Alira would come back to hand, champing her bit, alert now to every sound that could suggest monsters which were about to devour her.

Oh no! thought Lucy. *I have to get her to pass those dogs again to return to the stables!*

But she could not dwell on this because Alira was enervated and very much a handful.

Some benefits developed from these educative walks because Alira became braver and more tolerant of traffic. Ingrid began to alternate her schooling in the arena with hacks into the countryside but continued to experience a massive shy past the now predictable barking cacophony of the dogs and would then find Alira very strong and against the hand. Ingrid ventured to a ride along the road, with Lucy walking beside her, carrying a lead rope to attach in an emergency. They turned the other way out of the Equestrian Centre this time and Alira was extremely good and only a little unsettled by traffic, until they came to a small bridge over a stream. Automatically reassuring the horse with words and patting, Ingrid squeezed with her legs and encouraged her to go forward, anticipating some nervousness about the bridge – but now Alira planted herself in the road, transfixed and refusing to move. Head held high, neck muscles tensed into a rigid, iron slab, brown eyes bulging, showing the whites around the edge, the mare began to tremble and made a shrill snort down her nose, loud as a trumpet, abrupt and uncanny. Lucy tried to get her to move by pushing and patting her sweating shoulder, then attaching a lead rope to add more persuasion to go forward, for Ingrid's legs and hands were having little effect except to make the mare more agitated it seemed. Then the monsters came into view at the other side of the bridge. Cattle. Simple, black and white beasts, not so far from horses in their appearance, but they were the source of building panic in Alira. Lucy was adamant that they must get the young horse across the bridge, that Alira must not be allowed to get her own way and avoid the feared creatures, or she would never overcome her inexplicable terror.

Later, Ingrid and Lucy speculated that the scar on their horse's chest may have been a result of her being chased by cattle and consequently she associated them with pain and bleeding. But now, they just kept on trying to get her over the bridge, not to let her turn round and evade the beasts, which she must get used to, given that they are frequently encountered in the countryside and at shows.

Alira steadfastly refused, but after what seemed like an age and an encounter with an unsympathetic car driver, she took a few steps forward. "Good girl, good girl!" And then, in a turn of fate that seemed to be typical where this horse was concerned, the cattle decided to stampede forwards actually under the bridge, through the stream, perhaps to get away from flies.

Alira could not cope; she reared. Right up on her hind legs, vertical, on the slight gradient of the first part of the bridge, with Ingrid on top and the horrible risk of the horse going over backwards suddenly apparent. She would have gone, if it had not been for Lucy hanging onto the lead rein, pulling the horse forwards, trying to maintain her balance, using all her strength to get her down, save her daughter from injury and the horse too.

There were several horrible moments where Alira had lost her balance and her shoes were slipping on the tarmac. Then she fell backwards onto her hocks but was pulled forwards by Lucy onto her forelegs, Ingrid leaning as far forwards onto her horse's neck as she could, contributing to re-balancing the horse and avoiding catastrophe. Alira had scuffed hocks now and Lucy was gasping for breath. Ingrid was visibly shaken, pale and horrified at the horse's behaviour and the near disaster that would have happened had she gone over backwards.

Lucy's grandfather had been a horse dealer and even at an early age, her dad had been expected to help train the youngsters. Lucy had never known her grandfather but his words had echoed down the years and she had been told that if a horse rears, get rid of it. But she loved this horse already; her toxic, crazy energy, her subdued babyish self that contrasted sharply with the fiery wildness of the spirited, beautifully made little power pack who should have been a hand higher, a lot quieter, but could not possibly have been more charismatic, alluring, proud and fearsome.

Right now, Lucy and Ingrid were concentrating on walking the mare back to the stables, calming her adrenaline and keeping her steady. Incredibly, Lucy had got her over the bridge after the rearing episode, just leading her in hand which suggested that it was the cattle, not the bridge itself, which had frightened her. Ingrid remounted and then had an uncomfortable ride back as Alira jiggled and jogged sideways, head tossing and tail swishing. Ingrid sat quietly, her hands still and soft.

Such riding ability should be saved for a horse like this, Lucy thought, but immediately her mind clamoured. *What if Ingrid gets hurt?*

She was very close to both her daughters; could not bear the thought that she was complicit in a situation involving substantial risk to Ingrid. This was to be an agonising aspect of owning Alira; she was such a volatile horse. With Alira safely back in her stable, Lucy conveyed her thoughts to Ingrid, who would not hear of getting rid of her dream horse, passed it off as the mare being young and having had that incident with cattle, it would be unlikely to happen again.

Later that night, Ingrid went into the stable having settled Alira and simply stood with her and talked to her. She felt the solidity of her, the muscularity and the big, brown presence of her. She vowed not to be frightened by her extravagance of movement, her spirited rebellions; surely, those traits would make her a great dressage horse? They both went home exhausted after settling Alira down for the night, but then carried on as normal the next day, carefully caring for the grazed hocks.

The malevolent gossip of the other people who had horses at livery there did not subside and it was hard to be both so happy at finally owning a horse and feel so ostracised and resented at the same time. Gradually, it became obvious that the unfortunate episodes of the digger and the tractor were purposeful and designed to disrupt and antagonise both the horse and Lucy and Ingrid.

One day, the two women had made some enquiries about alternative stabling, which had been immediately reported back to Pamela, who was enraged! Her ducky voice did not enable her to shout, but she quacked extremely loudly about how affronted she was and suggested that they leave. Where could they take Alira now? They did not want to have to disrupt her training by moving her again, but who knows what tricks they would try next?

They did not have to wait long to find out. Ingrid was feeding Alira the following morning when she noticed something different about the scoop of feed she had taken out of the bag. She dug into the bag of Cool Mix; horse cubes, grain and flakes. Astonishingly, it was mixed with sand and gravel.

That was it. They were prepared to harm the horse in significant ways and it was intolerable to have this going on sneakily, covertly, not even knowing exactly who it was, so that they could confront them. They had to find somewhere else to keep Alira.

Chapter 7
The Stud Farm

Nobody who knew Pamela would let them stable Alira at their livery and in desperation James and Lucy drove up into the dales to look for somewhere. They tried farms and anywhere that looked as if it might have a stable, but to no avail. Just when Lucy was feeling tears of frustration pricking her eyes, they turned down a dusty track to a farmstead that appeared to have plenty of outbuildings and the evidence of people working in the yard. A warm and friendly chap was very sorry that he could not help…. But he did say, try up on the Lord Ainsty estate! Thrilled to have been given a lead, some hope, a prospect that there might be somewhere they could keep Alira, Lucy and James set off, back in the direction of home! Turning off the country lane they were navigating, they found themselves on a gravelled drive between neatly cut verges and proceeded between the tall aged trees which often suggest an estate of a traditional nature; here for sure there must be a wealthy landlord, with acres of well farmed land. A buzzard circled slowly, high, high up in the blue. They had passed a gatehouse at the entrance but there seemed to be nobody there. Now they came to a circular stone sign which announced: Ainsty Stud – Private.

The surroundings were elegant, ancient although well maintained and Lucy was thrilled – it was like a stud farm out of a story book, she could see a square concrete yard surrounded by neatly red painted half-doors – what is more, heads looked over some, with pricked ears, monitoring their arrival. She could not believe her good fortune when a woman approached them and in response to their query said, "Yes, we do livery here. The stud was used to breed thoroughbred horses and before that, horses to work on the land but now these are all livery stables."

Almost holding her breath, Lucy enquired whether they had any vacancies, to be told yes and asked if she wanted to see the stables. Delighted, Lucy affirmed that she would love to and was shown by Liz a capacious box in the corner of the yard which was available; it was big enough for a mare and foal, had a decent brick floor and the remnants of a previous occupant's straw bed. Liz quickly assured her that it would be cleaned out and made ready. Lucy could bring her horse as soon as she would like upon receipt of a month's livery fee in advance. Lucy was becoming aware that this latter was customary and they shook hands warmly, agreeing to bring Alira on the Saturday of that week, thereby giving Ingrid a chance to see the stable first and them both having time to transport Alira and her rapidly accumulating kit with them.

The items which they had had to buy already included, obviously, the saddle and bridle, but now, also a cavesson for lunging, a lunge line, lunge whip, a crop, grooming kit, feed, head collar as well as numerous ropes: because she kept chewing them! This would increase as winter came and Alira needed rugs. Also boots for her legs in case she over-reached when being schooled, over-reach boots themselves, which fit around the hoof and various other incidentals, such as grooming kit.

The Saturday dawned bright and sunny and they met Robin at the Equestrian Centre early. He was Ingrid's instructor from her younger days and had agreed to transport Alira in his horse trailer. The task of loading her loomed again! A much lower ramp and a stuffed hay net enticed her, but as ever, she was hesitant and kept running backwards away from the ramp.

"Let's try a bowl with some feed in!" suggested Ingrid and then succeeded in enticing her horse right into the trailer, with her head down, nose in the bucket, Ingrid going backwards, intending to reverse out of the jockey door at the front, which she did, forgetting that Alira would keep following her. Consequently, the mare's head went under the breast bar and when she threw her head up, realising she was in the trailer, she banged her poll hard on the bar.

"Oh no! cried Lucy, realising that it would further frighten Alira about trailers.

However, by this time, Robin and Ingrid had got the bar across behind her hind quarters and were quickly closing the ramp as Ingrid tied their special load up, gentling her continually.

They set off promptly, via the hills and dales that led up to Ainsty Stud, Lucy and Ingrid wondering how on earth Robin's old car would pull 500 kilogrammes of horse, plus the trailer, behind it, especially when they had to ascend a big, steep hill, Lucy looking anxiously behind to make sure the trailer was still following. They eventually found themselves driving down the long drive to their new livery yard, Lucy imagining stud grooms leading fine stallions along there in bygone days and picturing the beautiful Thoroughbred brood mares grazing the fields that fell away to their right, leggy foals standing close to their rounded bellies. Tall pines flanked the drive to the other side, the buzzard circled high in the distance. And suddenly, Alira's high shrill whinny changed the tranquillity and alerted some grazing horses that maybe would be her companions in the near future. Robin navigated the trailer across the bumpy gateway into the stable yard, passing the circular stone that announced: Ainsty Stud. He manoeuvred the trailer to a good position for unloading. Enthralled, Ingrid and Lucy jumped out, keen to unload their charge, who had actually travelled quite well.

Various people, whom they did not yet know, hung around as Alira clattered out onto the stable yard. Liz was there and hurried to show them their stable, so Lucy and Ingrid were oblivious to the gasps as the other livery owners saw Alira and were unable to hide their admiration.

"That's my dream horse, exactly what I want," Tracey muttered, but Liz was showing them the deep bed of straw she had put in the stable, explaining where the taps were and where the muck barrows were kept.

Robin took his leave from them and the others wandered away, while Ingrid tied a hay net up. Lucy tied Alira and was quietly grooming to settle her; the box was huge, a foaling box in the past probably and Alira had plenty of room to dash around it if permitted. Alira enjoyed being groomed but also objected strongly when brushed too firmly, stepping and swishing her tail, even kicking. A soft body brush was tolerated the best, so the dandy brush was reserved for tail and mane; the latter grew incorrectly on the left, refusing to lie on the right, customary side.

Eventually, Alira seemed to relax and the two women went home, soon to return and meet some of the other people, do hay nets, skip out the stable and so on. They made sure that they chatted to other people, determined not to alienate everybody this time. Rachel was a big woman with an abrupt manner who owned a large, bony old grey mare called Onyx, with which she mostly did hacking around the estate. These two had been there for years so could easily tell them the yard rules and customs. The woman who had coveted Alira appeared. She was small and dark, lived on the estate just near the stable yard and had an ex-racehorse at livery, which it transpired, she hardly ever rode. A pleasant mother and daughter had a bay gelding called Scott, which they evented. Then there was Betsy, a passionate advocate of Western style riding, who put a huge saddle with a high pommel on her tall, dark horse, then rode away with no bit in his mouth, just a halter and reins of plaited rope. They were introduced to Tim, who worked on the estate, a man of few words and a manner of deference more suited to the last century.

The following morning was dull and damp as Lucy made her way to do morning stables. The countryside was in glorious summer regalia, but rain dripped from the trees and the sun was well hidden by bulbous grey clouds which rested above the hilltops. Passing the gatehouse where Liz and her family lived, she imagined Liz cooking on a big range in a large kitchen adjoining a 'best room' where a comfortable sofa enabled visitors to sit back and admire old paintings of prizewinning racehorses bred at the stud. But then at the back, there would be a utility room where Liz would take off her muddy boots and leave her horse kit. Her husband was the gamekeeper so perhaps would come in there with dogs and wet overcoats, maybe a brace of pheasants for dinner.

Lucy drove on past the high trees, which she now realised hid a margin of woodland scrub before the fields dropped away to the North. To the South were the fields which the livery horses used and Lucy wondered nervously where Alira would go. Liz had assured her that horses only ever went out in a small group. There was no mixing of mares and geldings and no group consisted of more than five horses in total. Lucy saw a group of horses with a donkey, but then realised it was not a donkey, rather a small cob with a hogged mane and a flat back, alongside the big gelding which had the Western style rider. Lucy speculated that the other horse she could see with them was the eventer.

Arriving in the yard, she saw Alira's dark face with ears pricked and eyes alert, looking out over her half door. Whilst tending to feeding and mucking out she saw Liz and asked where she could turn her mare out.

"Bring her down to the bottom stables and I'll show you," was the brusque retort.

Lucy began to realise that Liz's manner was abrupt even when she was being friendly, but could not help liking and slightly admiring her too, more so as she chatted to her and learned of a lifelong history of riding horses, including racing in point-to-points, retraining racehorses and breaking in young horses.

Lucy and her horse walked downhill through some woods and Alira walked beside her, they turned off the track and reached some buildings, consisting of a small block of stables and a lunge pen, after which a gate led into a field where four horses grazed. Alira tensed as Lucy led her through the mud, turned her round and let her go. The four mares advanced to investigate their new friend.

For a while, they circulated round the field as a group and then came back to the gate, the four tight together, Alira gracefully trotting around the outside of the group, head held high, anxiety writ large upon her body.

"She needs to stop moving," Lucy pointed out.

"But, boy, can she move," breathed Liz.

Lucy was stunned that this no-nonsense woman was visibly impressed by her horse. They watched a while longer until the other mares' desire to graze overcame their interest in arranging a new hierarchy in the field, Alira calmed down too and started to eat. Lucy breathed a sigh of relief and left to go to work.

She could not wait to call Ingrid that evening, as it was her daughter's turn to do 'evening stables' and she wanted to find out if their mare was unscathed, had not been kicked, bitten or hurt herself in some other way.

Ingrid's voice was reassuring, "No, she was fine, just bitten all over by flies."

Discussion ensued. A flysheet and hood would be purchased. The next day was Ingrid's first ride on Alira at the new premises; this took place in a very small ménage, levelled out into the hillside and surrounded by a wooden fence. The mare behaved well and Ingrid was able to guide her carefully on the inside track, for the specialised surface fell away sharply at the edge and could easily result in losing a step.

Life went on with Alira at Ainsty Stud. They trained her to have her feet picked out without kicking, to stand and have her legs hosed, to partially overcome her fear of the building known as the 'Wash Box'. Ingrid rode her up to the Gatehouse and schooled her in the ménage. Lucy led her out in hand on the nights when Ingrid was busy at work, introducing her to a lot of things that she was afraid of. Then the cattle came.

Lucy and Ingrid took her together, wearing a cavesson, with a rein at either side, just to look at them from the other side of the fence. The piercing snort came straightaway and the cattle were curious, so they came and crowded up to the fence. They must have looked like poor Alira's worst nightmare; she tried to spin, she ran back, she had diarrhoea, she reared and tried to bolt. No amount of calming talk or gentle touch mitigated her horror and after a monumental battle just to keep her with them, Lucy and Ingrid took her back to the yard. She was like a coiled spring, jogging sideways all the way, their arms were aching with the effort of holding her.

Not long after this, the cattle were moved to a field just below the ménage! Ingrid and Alira were now creating a partnership when Alira was under saddle, showing a harmony that was a joy to watch. Whilst schooling, Ingrid taught her to be responsive to leg aids, to do transitions from one pace to the next when asked by leg and hand, generally to ignore distractions, just listen to her rider and not play up.

Incredibly, by working her initially at the top of the ménage and gradually widening the circle, Alira worked while a bull lowed in his deep rumbling voice below and cows with calves grazed across the field, occasionally walking across to the water trough to drink, thereby coming nearer to the lower end of the schooling area. The extent of Alira's fear of cattle made Lucy and Ingrid think this good behaviour was a cause for celebration, the beginnings of a partnership which might compete in dressage competitions!

Chapter 8
Horsey Men

Ingrid had sourced a farrier for Alira, because the one that people used at the Equestrian Centre was not a man they would entertain. They had observed him shoeing a horse, whilst another animal across the way was banging its door, clearly impatient to be fed, taken out or at least get attention.

After telling it to 'Shut up!' a few times, the man had lost his temper and hurled a metal horseshoe at this horse. Such appalling behaviour for someone who has to do the intricate work involved in attaching a metal shoe to horses' feet, tapping in nails just centimetres away from sensitive tissue, necessitating patience and calmness, particularly with young horses was inexcusable. Kevin, the farrier who they chose upon the recommendation of Ingrid's ex-instructor, was a quiet, young man who was undemonstrative, but it was easy to see that horses instinctively trusted him. He was also very good at his job, using hot shoes prepared in his mobile forge, ensuring shoes were balanced and true, noting the horse's way of going and the structure of their feet. When he shod Alira, he quickly noted that she had small hind feet, which was not something that he identified as a problem, but over the years, this small fact may have indeed been significant in a number of ways.

Robin was the ex-instructor who had taught Ingrid while she was still at school, getting her to ride Copper and develop a non-descript riding school cob into a dressage horse. He was an athletic man who still rode horses himself, having been a point-to-point jockey when he was younger. He loved horses and life and was convinced health and longevity stemmed from a positive mental attitude, eating a big breakfast, a smaller lunch and a tiny supper, plus the use of Aloe Vera, a gel purported to aid digestion and do numerous other amazing things.

Robin had no fear of any horse, rode fearlessly in steeplechases in his youth and now in competitive long-distance rides, but he was unable to get past one of Alira's tantrums. This particular day, he appeared when Ingrid was trying to get her to work in a field, as opposed to the confines of the little arena which they had used up until now. The wind blew fresh and cold across the open fields and Alira's face was a picture of fury; her ears were back, her neck was arched, she chomped the bit and in no way looked compliant. Alira resisted Ingrid's attempts to make her listen, she set her neck so that she could hold her bit and ignore Ingrid's hands, her sides were tense and hard, she shortened her body and Ingrid's legs felt wooden resistance as she attempted to get her to move forwards and stretch.

Robin materialised in the field, standing in the middle, suggesting, "Push her on! Move her neck, turn her!"

His enthusiastic shouting appeared to be ignored, but it was because Alira was just not responding to her rider.

"Push her on!" yelled Robin.

Ingrid was sure that this would result in a bolt and with no feeling in her horse's mouth, she had no way of stopping her. "All right, stop and rein her back. That might get her to listen."

Ingrid tried but Alira fought back with an ominous half-rear, challenging her rider's authority and shaking her nerve. Robin was getting exasperated in a good-humoured way; he knew this young woman was a gifted rider but could not see why she appeared nervous of her horse.

"Get her moving! Use that electric bottom of yours!"

Crossly, Ingrid said, "You get on and do it!"

Robin obliged, Ingrid slipped off her horse and he got on with ease, gathering up the reins with his customary slight smile on his face, clearly confident. He had indeed ridden many, many horses in his lifetime as a horseman and saw no reason why he couldn't deal with this one. He slowly negotiated enough obedience from Alira to navigate an approximate large circle, but the movement was punctuated by half-rears, napping and turns in the opposite direction. The smile was replaced by a look of grim determination, but it was not long before the mare stood in front of Ingrid again and Robin dismounted for her to continue. Robin watched in silence as Ingrid experienced similar misbehaviour; however, she succeeded in getting her to trot briefly. Disheartened, Ingrid took her to the gate, where she started running back, then stood up on her hind legs as her rider leaned down to open it. Ingrid had had enough and slipped down off her mare's untrustworthy back, to lead her disconsolately through the trees.

Alira's temperament was going to be difficult to work with, but the alacrity with which she could stand on her hind legs was testament to the power and ease of her movement. She was beautiful when she was angry but so frustrating.

Robin dismissed Lucy's anxious questions when they arrived back in the yard. "All young horses rear, she'll get over it."

He seemed to have absolute confidence in the two of them being able to work with this obstreperous horse! They did. The summer wore on and autumn began to create a chaos of colours amongst the abundant trees on the estate. The cold wind was biting and the mare hated bad weather, no doubt longing for the softer climate of the South where she was raised. But Ingrid rode her in the ménage, Lucy standing in the middle, encouraging, praising, suggesting, trying to get her daughter to develop a confidence in this stunning little horse, that she did not actually feel herself.

"Mrs Hennedy!" Lucy heard her name called one day as she watched Ingrid ride Alira.

Melvyn was an old friend, a veteran of racehorses and event riding, a polite, enthusiastic horseman of the old school, brimming with stories of equestrian feats and various experiences. He doffed his hat and kissed Lucy enthusiastically on both cheeks, his height and strength making her own seem slight.

Lucy straightened her own hat now and responded to his questions. "Yes, we are at livery here. She came from down South, she is bred from the line of Rubenstein, but she has Furioso in there too, as you can see!"

Melvyn watched the feisty little mare do trot to canter transitions, her rider sitting still and deep in the saddle, but pulled slightly forward by the strength of Alira leaning on her hands, keen, forward-going, but strongly fighting against the hands that held her.

"We are struggling with her a bit and she is really difficult out in the field."

Ingrid came to them now, bringing her mount to a standstill alongside, the mare tossing her head, sending foam flying, but friendly and keen to explore Melvyn's pockets, once he had laid a reassuring hand on her. He carefully ran his big hands over her quarters and all four legs, then came back to stroke her arched neck.

"My, you're a pretty one, eh, my lass? Where did you find her?"

"Oh, we had to go right down to the South, where she was bred," replied Lucy.

Discussion followed and Melvyn was adamant that what she needed was long reining to make her soften her jaw and accept the bit; it would give her confidence and quieten her down. He was very keen to help two such lovely ladies and perhaps be their knight in shining armour, who resolved the problems they were having with this young horse which looked so full of potential. A kiss on the cheek for Ingrid and two for Lucy, then he must be going, but not before he had checked over Alira when untacked and back in the stable. He did a lot of equine remedial therapy, concentrating in particular on horses' backs. Feeling the mare's broad, thick spine, he was delighted with her, could find no fault. Lucy and Ingrid were very pleased and content to listen to stories of the days when Alira's current home was a Thoroughbred stud.

"They raced them too, you know. I remember a stallion who stood here, we took him up to Newcastle, he was a broth of a horse, stood sixteen hands high and bite you soon as look at you. He did not want to load that day" – Lucy and Ingrid looked at each other at this point – "and it took four men to get him up the ramp, one at his head and three behind, we almost carried him up it! At the other end, we let the ramp down and he *shot* out, broke his head collar and cantered off. Aye, but he ran a good race that day. I tell you we had a good celebration that night!"

Arrangements were made that Melvyn would come to long-rein Alira the following day and he would start in the field, overcome their problems. Lucy was hesitant, but then thought that maybe it was an obvious answer; get the mare going freely forwards without somebody on her back and she would be safely held by such a strong man. She herself would not be able to be there due to work commitments; however, Ingrid would be there to help.

Ainsty Stud was high in the hills, but higher land escalated beyond it, eventually giving way to the moorland tops. That autumn, they learnt that its predominant weather condition was fog. Ingrid drove up to the stud that day to find herself enveloped in swirling grey dampness, people, trees and buildings became vague shapes, indistinct in the swirling mass of water droplets, even sounds were muffled by the dense fog. Ingrid got her mare ready, fed, mucked out, watered, groomed. Melvyn arrived and carefully contrived long reins that ran from the bit and through the leathers on the saddle, so he could walk behind, getting her walking on and forwards into her bit. Initially, Ingrid walked at her head; led her down through the avenue of trees to the fields. Then Melvyn took over, talking away to Alira.

Ingrid watched from a slight distance, becoming partly dismayed and partly amused as it became obvious that this man, who was so experienced and so confident, could not manage Alira either. She planted four hooves firmly in the ground, looked warily behind her, not predisposed to understand what was required of her. Eventually, a sharper tone and a tap on the behind propelled her forwards, but not in a straight line. She passaged sideways (Ingrid made a mental note that she did not need teaching that part of dressage!). She shied at invisible monsters behind tufts of grass, she plunged forwards, fighting the bit, defying the hands that held her, pushing from those low, now slightly capped, hocks. Melvyn let her go forwards but walk was too slow for this 'Daughter of Attitude' and she packed her body short, trying to canter at the man's fast walking speed, then when she was not allowed to go, up she went into a rear, her new default setting. Then down to plant herself again, paw the ground to show her frustration, then repeat that performance again.

They proceeded in this manner, slowly up the field, Melvyn now florid, breathless, embarrassed at his inability to get the mare to behave. For she was not accepting the bit at any time, being either behind it so that the reins hung in dangerously low loops, or fighting against it, pulling like a train, then leaping forwards as if she could escape the restraint of the light snaffle.

Whatever next? thought Ingrid. *Would she bolt, what if she reared and went over, why was she being so uncompromising?*

55

Melvyn suggested they take her into the ménage to maybe help her settle into his long reining; Ingrid shut the gate for them as the mist swallowed man and horse and she became aware of a low bellowing from the bull calling to his cows, invisible in the fog below. That did it. Without Ingrid riding her or Lucy at her head, the feared animals were just too much to deal with, only a strange man behind her and mist writhing across towards her.

Only through his wealth of experience and surprising dexterity for so large a man did Melvyn avoid being knocked aside by Alira or her getting a leg over the long rein and entanglement ensuing. For she shot sideways, snorted, flew forwards, ran back into Melvyn and ultimately tried to flee, head in the air, shaking her mane and leaping as if possessed by demons.

Ingrid ran to her head and managed to grab her, while Melvyn also came forwards to hold her, the long reins still around her quarters, both of them telling her to, "Whoa, whoa, whoa."

The session of what was meant to be training ended in the fog, Melvyn for once quiet, unable to understand why this fiery little horse would not come under his control; he never offered to help to train her again.

Men who like horses often seemed to like women in jodhpurs and boots, women who are usually fit, strong and athletic. Lucy and Ingrid were tall, with Scandinavian good looks, had a dark, charismatic, unmistakably special horse and men would look and look again. Vet, farrier, friend or associate, they all became very interested in Alira Compliquer, but quite in awe of her too.

Chapter 9
Pocket Rocket

The land of the estate was beautiful with big green fields, punctuated by tussocks of rough grass which the horses did not eat, giving a variation of shades of green, some slightly longer grass giving shelter to birds, which could find even better habitats in the thick hedges. Not all fields were divided by hedges, many were flanked by traditional grey stone walls, solid and weathered by many decades of wind, rain and snow, softened by mosses and lichen that clung to the irregular shapes of the stones. Trees provided shelter but also harboured flies in the summer months, their numerous heights and shapes completing the effect of a landscape which fitted the elegance of a rural environment which had changed little over the years.

Liz rotated the use of her grazing land and soon Alira moved fields to a long field at the other side of the avenue of trees, which she shared with the big grey mare Onyx, a bay mare 'Scandal', an old chestnut mare 'Pisces' and a grey pony who was on holiday until his owners returned to collect him. The grey pony was small and non-threatening, so Alira quickly became quite attached to him. Lucy and Ingrid made friends with the different horses' owners but had to tread carefully.

Scandal's owners were also a mother and daughter, but neither rode very often so their mare was out in the field for long stretches of time. Eventually they would come, drive their car between the long avenue of trees to then emerge in high-heeled sandals and flimsy dresses. They would tip a large bag of carrots over the gate and then complain when squealing and kicking ensued, the other horses having sensed a treat and coming to fight for a share. Inevitably, Alira got kicked and there was a wound to clean with salt and water, antiseptic cream to apply and then the worry that it would leave a scar. Alira was young and healed well, but was clueless about herd mentality, not always respecting the Alpha mare, who at this time was Onyx. Alira seemed happy enough to graze alongside the little pony, Basil; however, turning her out in the field was becoming increasingly problematic. The velocity with which Alira launched away from the gateway was unbelievable and she had little regard for her handler as she shot away; attempts to teach her to wait made things worse, because she would fight so hard to get away that she would ultimately win, then gallop harder upon release. Her gallop across the field was as if she had been released from a starting gate, carrying her straight past the other horses to the distant boundary fence, where she would slow, then canter round in a big loop to join the other horses and graze. The field caused her more anxiety when a small flock of sheep began to share it, but she settled with them in a day or two. She became notorious for her galloping when released and soon attracted a surreptitious audience.

Elaine owned the gelding which Lucy had thought was a donkey on the day they first came; she often seemed to materialise through the trees after they had let Alira go and Elaine started to call their mare the 'Pocket Rocket'. Lucy became friends with Elaine, who would tell many tales of the amazing exploits of Monty, her horse, who had the size and shape of a mule and was every bit as stubborn. But she loved him and with her warm Scottish brogue and easy laughter, she would make Lucy laugh and make both of them late for work with her chatter, but it was such a delight to have friendships at this yard, in stark contrast to the vitriol of the Equitation Centre previously.

Lucy and Ingrid got to know the others and soon felt that they fitted in quite well; Liz was perhaps more of a challenge to befriend. She was in charge and everyone knew it, but Lucy could not help but like her stoic attitude and kind manner with horses, even if she was sometimes abrupt in conversation. She let Lucy and Ingrid know that their horse often chose to gallop during the day, not just a play around but a determined flat-out circuit of the field, sometimes several times, interspersed with skidding to a halt, head high and snorting, only to go again, with seemingly endless stamina.

With autumn came winds and rain that lashed the hills, days where the cold wind cut like a knife and Ingrid announced that they must go and buy their horse a rug, for their mare was fine skinned and grew little hair. Lucy was cautious for she knew that putting rugs on too soon can inhibit the growth of winter coat, but when one day the mare came in chilled and cold she was keen to purchase one too.

Soon, Alira was going out into the field with a red rug pulled tightly over her powerful shoulders and hanging nicely at her sides, now being heralded as the 'Red Peril' as she sported it around the field at speed. Ingrid gave Alira more work to calm her down, riding her every day when she could, but it seemed in no way to reduce the energy expended in the field. Taking her out of her stable in the morning before they went to work, she would seem keen and excited to go to the field and this excitement increased as they passed through the avenue of trees, building up as she neared the gateway, she would be right on her toes and getting stronger as she went.

One typical autumnal day, when Lucy took her down to the field, the route had become more mysterious and threatening for Alira, due to constant movement and rustling in the undergrowth beneath the trees, terrifying until the monster materialised and invoked a massive shy. It would be one of many groups of pheasants newly released for the shooting season, hundreds having been reared in pens around the estate. Groups of them crept amongst the vegetation, dockings, nettles and brambles, their scratching and pecking adding to the already mysterious creaking and sighing of the trees above and Alira was like a war horse ready to charge, except her charge would be away from this feared place!

Lucy had aching shoulders as she led her, but never complained, aware how privileged they were to have a spirited horse like this, admiring the curve of her neck, the shine of her coat, the wideness of her eyes set above a broad cheek which tapered elegantly towards nostrils now flared as she prepared for 'flight or fight'. All that was happening was the fight because flight was constrained by her owner! Alira looked as if she was pulling Cleopatra's chariot, not being quietly led to her field.

"Come steady girl, whoa, my lady, good girl, you're all right" Lucy reassured her in vain and told herself to hang on, hoping that a pheasant did not actually fly up.

She was slightly relieved when they got to the field gate, but by now Alira was prancing and cantering on the spot; letting her go when they were in the field was fraught with difficulty anyway. She used the usual routine, through the gate, "Come around," was the command and then Alira allowed her to shut the gate. But now as Lucy's hands moved slowly towards the head collar the mare was becoming tense, her neck hardened, Lucy was being as quick as she could now, the buckle was undone, the great leap came when the head collar was undone, but this time it was not to veer away, but to go around Lucy! The mare's powerful shoulder was against her, those flying hooves inches from her feet!

"Get away!!" shouted Lucy and shoved at the brown form that seemed almost on top of her.

This transformed the velocity into a trajectory, taking the troubled horse away across the field, hoof beats thundering on the dry ground, a racehorse trying to reach the finishing line, not a dressage horse gracefully joining the other horses!

This became the customary mode of departure when Alira was released into the field and the gallop became more dramatic; the tendency to try to round up whoever was letting her go made it progressively more treacherous. She seemed to have fear of the gateway itself and wanted whichever owner was there to come with her, not to stay in the threatening gateway!

One day, Liz was returning from her lower stables by the lunge pen and came past the field gate, hence chanced to watch Alira be released. The horse shot away down the short side of the oblong field, turned on her haunches in the bottom corner in order to have a straight gallop across the diagonal, heading for the far top corner – a good distance, for it was a big field. This time, she exceeded all previous gallops; she lowered herself towards the ground, shortened her body and went for it as if her life depended on it. The ground reverberated with the thunder of her hooves and Elaine, Lucy, Ingrid and Liz watched in astonished silence.

Somehow, in the top corner she stopped. "It's mad!" shouted Liz, referring to Alira. "It's mad!" as she turned and carried on her way up between the trees.

She was hard of hearing so tended to shout, but Lucy and Ingrid were somewhat taken aback by this verdict on their horse which was pronounced so emphatically. Throughout the years that followed, they would remember these words and wonder at times whether Liz was right.

One Saturday morning, they were turning out Onyx for her owner, so Ingrid led her into the field first, turning to hand the gate to Lucy so she could bring Alira through, when Alira shied at something in the undergrowth by the gate. Lucy had no problem restraining her as she had done many times before, but this time she whipped round, knocking Lucy off her feet and she was going, no delay – but Lucy would not let go.

Determined that the horse would not be harmed, she hung grimly onto the rope, as a consequence being dragged across the lane on her right hip.

She was vaguely aware of pain and then shouting, which was Ingrid, of course, "Let go! Let go!" and then she had to let go, for Alira was at full gallop and Lucy risked serious injury.

Now they would find out where and how far she went when she had freedom. Initially she headed for Liz's stables and galloped into there, where Liz tried to catch her and failed, for she again whipped round and was off, back the way she had come. Liz was on her feet by this time and thought she would catch her or stop her as she came back, but the mare was at full gallop and even attempts to divert her failed, Liz waving her arms, standing in her way.

The horse had no intention of stopping and would have gone through or over her. Lucy had to dodge out of the way and Alira carried on with her headlong flight, now back in the direction of the yard; but there was a T-junction at the top of the lane, where if she turned left she would quickly be onto the road. Ingrid and Lucy watched helplessly as she flew towards it and held their breath as she arrived at the junction as if she was going straight on, but then whipped to her right, amazingly not losing footing on the tarmac, now vanishing towards the stable yard and its downward sloping concrete yard. Would she stay on her feet?

Ingrid checked that Lucy was still in one piece and legged it back up the lane after her horse. She could run fast and soon was out of sight to Lucy as she made her way painfully and slowly after her, at one point sitting down on a tree stump for a rest.

Liz came past with Tricia and said quite kindly, "Are you okay?" Lucy blushed with embarrassment as she realised Liz had seen all that happened but was grateful for her concern.

"Yeah, I'll be fine!" was Lucy's reply, anxious to seem strong to this woman who had probably fallen off horses at speed over fences. "Just wondering if Alira is!"

They arrived back in the yard to find Alira with Ingrid in the wash box; having caught her, Ingrid had not wanted to give her the reward of going back into her stable. Careful scrutiny revealed Alira to be completely unscathed, so this time they took her to the field together, a rein at each side and for once, she did not even canter when they let her go, just some elevated trot across to Basil. Lucy's leg and hip were blooming into shades of purple, she was very glad that she had strong bones and nothing had broken.

Leaves began to fall and the pathways were hushed by a deep carpet of them, Alira began to relax on her journey to the field and once in the field but was still difficult in the gateway. Rain came too and turned the gateway into a muddy puddle, which widened and deepened as horses were brought in at night, every night. The soil here was a heavy clay, even though the land was set beneath a limestone escarpment; this meant Alira turned away through the mire of very holding mud, using her hocks to leap away and they feared mightily for her tendons. She was sturdy and had eight inches of bone, but even so, they cringed each day that she did it, started putting boots on to protect her from strain and over-reach, but boots can only do so much.

Mud fever followed, she had thin skin and grew hardly any coat or feathering; this land had been used for horses for decades and their young horse as yet had little resistance to the mud fever that is a consequence of wet legs and muddy conditions. All that winter they struggled to keep it under control, washing her legs when she came in, using copious amounts of kitchen roll to ensure that they were completely dry, then applying cream to the red, swollen pustules on her lower legs.

Even with all this care, the mud fever became infected and they had to get some antibiotic from the vet. They battled with it all that winter, after which Alira developed immunity and it never troubled her again. Lucy and Ingrid did not know that this would happen and felt despair at times, because all the gateways were deep in mud by now. The bonus was that having to wash her legs made her get used to the hosepipe; at first, she thought it was a snake, refused to stand still and threatened to break away, but with there being two of them they gradually got her to stand and eat hay whilst one of them hosed and the other stopped her from casting about or backing up. Soon she saw it as routine and never forgot that lesson.

Liz came to them one night. "They're going in the top field tomorrow, so she will be in there for the next few weeks."

"Okay," replied Ingrid, "There are cattle next door to that field, aren't there?"

Liz laughed. "Yes, it will help her get used to them."

Logical, in theory, but when was Alira likely to conform to theory? The following morning was Saturday, so while Ingrid mucked out, Lucy decided to take Alira to see the cattle again and spend time familiarising her, give her some treats and be really patient until she relaxed.

The cattle were already by the fence when Lucy led her into what was to be her new field, across towards them, but not too near at first. These were smaller beasts than the others she had contended with and thankfully, the wind was blowing their smell away from Alira. Lucy felt triumphant as she gradually coaxed the mare nearer and nearer to them. The cattle were looking through the fence now and woman and horse were standing side by side, with Alira relatively calm, nodding her head for her next treat and being warmly accoladed by Lucy.

She held her by the bridle and they had both relaxed, Lucy was stroking her neck, when Alira struck out with her foreleg, impatient and as ever, extravagant, raising it high and bringing towards the ground with force; unfortunately, it caught Lucy above her kneecap and tears of pain stung her eyes. She did not alter her stance for fear of spoiling the mare's behaviour, just held herself rigid until the pain subsided a little.

Soon after that, she decided the cattle lesson had been long enough and she could not wait to tell Ingrid how well it had gone. She had not anticipated how Alira's adrenaline had been building up or how much her fear would increase with the cattle behind her, perhaps, in her equine mind, in a position to chase. The minute Lucy turned her she was in the air and fighting to go. With the pain in her knee, Lucy simply could not hold her, the horse bolted down the field at a flat-out gallop. Lucy heard the reins snap as they tangled round a foreleg and then bang, the mare crashed into the wall in the far bottom corner of the field, her headlong flight rendering her unable to stop and of course, she was as yet unaware of the parameters of this field.

She cantered off again as if unharmed and Lucy hobbled after her, eventually catching her and taking her painfully back to the yard. What she thought had been a success had been a disaster; however, the horse, amazingly, did not seem damaged from her collision with the wall, better it was that than a wire fence, which she would have charged through and perhaps ripped herself open.

But the cattle were there in the next field and Alira had to be turned out while they went to work. Liz had been asked but was not prepared to make another field available, so they just had to hope that the presence of the other mares would prevent Alira from bolting through any fences. Thankfully, it did and Alira was initially, grazing calmly with the others.

This lasted for a few days and to their great relief, all seemed well. Ingrid rode and found Alira fresh, excitable, but sound and happy to work. She worked on the 'Scales of Training', which are as follows: rhythm, suppleness, contact, impulsion, straightness and collection. She had freedom in her paces, which gave her fluency and therefore rhythm, she was naturally athletic so Ingrid could work on her suppleness, but she was temperamental, unbalanced, flighty and unpredictable.

Once Ingrid had started a project, she never gave up, so she carried on, patiently working her, improving her, calming her; getting her to do transitions, trying to achieve obedience, seeking fluency and balance, trying to get her to accept the bit with an even contact. Hacking her out was supposed to increase her confidence, but was quite alarming for both of them. She objected to the presence of a pram one day and almost turned herself inside out. Ingrid stuck to her like glue; she had the ability to rarely move in the saddle but hated the half rear she would produce and the alacrity with which she could turn and twist and veer.

Lucy had barely had time to reflect since they brought her into their possession, she was so busy and the minute her head hit the pillow at night she was asleep, worn out with just her share of the work, while Ingrid did the most and was still giving 100% to her occupation and social life! They both loved their mare already, so beautiful, already attached to them and very trainable in the stable, she was responding to them and behaving in a much more respectful way. James occasionally would be up at the yard to lend a hand, especially if there was a heavy job, like unloading hay or bags of shavings. Otherwise, he was a 'horse widow', meaning he hardly saw his wife, due to her work and all the time she spent at the stables!

Now another problem was developing. Since going into the new field, Alira had another crazy habit, which was in complete contrast to her galloping. She would position herself by the gate and stand there all day. From being turned out until Lucy or Ingrid came at night, she would be there, never leaving her position. This was a major problem, because she was not eating or drinking, she was stood in the mud exacerbating the mud fever, and she must have been cold, for the weather seemed to be more wintery by the day. Nothing would persuade her to be elsewhere, if led away she would immediately return. This led to them paying Liz to bring her in after a couple of hours, but that in turn meant that she spent long hours in the stable and was wild when Ingrid wanted to ride her, full of energy and resistant to being schooled. She was unsafe to hack because of the number of ghosts the young horse conjured up in her mind and displayed excessive fear to and she started to develop a bad habit.

Recently, Tricia's horse had been in the stable quite a lot and it appeared that it was a wind-sucker, in other words it took hold of something with its teeth, then sucked in air with a loud gulping noise. Alira observed this and thought she might do it too, grabbing hold of the top of her door and straining to swallow some air, which was a bad idea for a prospective dressage horse. This could become a constant habit and led to the development of muscles in the wrong places on the neck, as well as causing digestive problems and weird noises in the gut.

Quickly, Ingrid adorned the door with some nasty smelling stuff designed for the purpose of making it unpleasant to get hold of, which prevented Alira from doing it; but it suggested that she was bored, maybe anxious and also hungry. The obvious thing would be to give her more to eat, but more to eat resulted in more energy, which was not what she needed! Haylage had far too much protein, so the search was on for an old-fashioned farmer who made small bales of hay on land that was not too rich and the hay needed to have been baled without getting too much rain on it to make it dusty. Alira had already been troubled with a cough, which vanished as soon as they stopped using straw for her to lie on and replaced it with shavings; more expensive but Alira seemed designed to need money spending on her! Horses usually love to eat and the art of feeding one is to find the balance needed to keep them looking well without putting too much unmanageable energy in them. This was to be a constant issue for Alira, who utilised her food most effectively, yet was very oral, liking to chew so requiring a good amount of forage to eat at.

Lucy started to lunge Alira before Ingrid got on and rode her, sometimes utilising the ménage and at other times taking her down to the lunge pen where Liz's stables were. This was designed to expend some of her energy and then perhaps calm her in order to make her easier to ride and more disposed to listen to her rider's aids. The mare found these interludes very exciting and usually went a great deal faster than she should have done until she settled into a rhythmic trot or canter – that was a delight to watch.

When Lucy had a rare minute to reflect, perhaps when she was letting the mare graze for a minute on the lead rein, she marvelled at how her whole identity had changed. From being tightly bound up with the place she worked and the frustrations of the modern education system, to being a horse owner, to have a dream, as yet indeterminate, but just a belief that this horse was special, this mare was magic. That she and Ingrid were on a journey and were fulfilling their dream of being horse owners, of being part of an incredibly privileged group of people, lucky enough to own a horse, but also dedicated enough, in most cases, to work fantastically hard to give a horse everything it needs, tend to it day and night, work all hours to gain the money to pay for it. Far from being a glamorous world, a lot of it was mucking out, scraping mud from filthy beasts, washing, cleaning, mending; but then there were those moments of sheer joy, watching the horse move, admiring its beauty, interacting in a way that led to understanding between person and horse.

Ingrid had the joy of riding, of training, the increased harmony that results when horse understands human and responds, the difficult task of negotiating obedience with Alira. The mare could not be told, just asked, and when Ingrid felt the response, felt the surge of those powerful quarters, the fluency of her movement, the stretch of her walk, the bounce of her trot and the swing of her canter, she was absorbed, transported, into a world that involved just her and the hoof beats. Her and the snort and sweat of the animal, her and the controlled power that sometimes defied her, sometimes frightened her, but always thrilled her. Their lives had been taken over by the ownership of Alira Compliquer and nothing else could get in the way of their ambitions for her. What were those ambitions? For Lucy, to care for this horse so that it was safe, healthy, looked fit, well presented and happy; for Ingrid, to train this horse to do dressage and prove herself in the arena.

Chapter 10
The Big Snow

When the snow came, it came fast and furious, deep, blanketing land already frozen by the onset of winter cold that had started early this year, grasping the land in an icy grip. Not for years had there been so much snow and it came in that first winter, when Lucy and Ingrid were still trying to prove to themselves that they could care for a horse and still go to work and live their everyday lives. Alira was four or five miles away from the town where they both lived, along up-and-down lanes that twisted and turned the way up into the hills to get to the young horse, a thin-skinned Warmblood from the South of England who was used to mellow skies and moderate temperatures.

Lucy had a small car, quite old, just a general run around and now they had to contemplate dealing with all this ice and snow! The first decision that they made that day was to go together so that they could help each other and only one vehicle needed to be involved. Lucy was game to drive in the snow; she had plenty of experience from living on an outlying farm in her youth. This was different though. They had to get to work after they had dealt with their horse!

They set off at an early hour, which felt like the crack of dawn, only dawn had not arrived yet and they could only see snow everywhere in the headlights after they had scraped and cleaned their way into the car. The car was freezing, the cold outside biting; much as they were well wrapped up in layers of clothing, they still shivered. They struggled to negotiate the roads immediately above the town, then got going along a gritted stretch of road before turning up into the hills. These roads were untreated, the snow was deeper and the edges of the road were indistinct, merging into frosted, laden hedges, which blended into massive whiteness stretching to the horizons, now being slowly revealed by the rising daylight. Cautiously they proceeded, sliding, skidding, sometimes on top of the snow and sometimes grinding through it, finding traction on the road.

Next, the greatest challenge appeared. They were looking at a long dip down to a small bridge over a tributary which rushed towards the river, with an equally steep ascent on the other side.

Ingrid spoke from within her fur hood, "We have to get to our horse! She will be safe in her stable but she's probably hungry, maybe cold and perhaps frightened, she might never have seen snow before!"

Lucy spoke softly to herself, "Don't think too much, put it in third gear to hold it down the hill, do not touch the brakes!"

They advanced down the hill, gathering speed now, Lucy correcting every deviation of the car with minimal, sensitive, immediate intervention on the steering wheel – "Up the other side, into fourth gear, less traction, speed will carry her up the first bit then accelerate." – Ingrid let out a shriek as the little vehicle bounced and twisted, buffeted by the ruts in the snow as it careered up the hill.

"We've made it!"

Lucy's jubilation was short-lived as they realised the road to the gates of Ainsty Stud still had a gradual upward gradient, so down a gear again and they gently proceeded up the hill, with just enough power to keep going, a lower gear now, but very light acceleration or the wheels just started to spin.

Steely concentration and sheer determination got them to the gates of Ainsty Stud. Now the drive to negotiate, with its virgin snow creaking under the wheels and still more careful steering, to make sure they did not end up in the deeper snow on the verge. They left the car by the stone wheel sign, not risking getting stuck in the yard. What a relief it was, Lucy was triumphant, but Ingrid slightly pale and traumatised by her mother's boldness at the wheel!

Straight to Alira now though. There she was, a little way back from the door, suspicious about the strange, cold atmosphere and muffled sounds. The yard was a sloping ice rink, treacherous as they both advanced with filled hay nets.

Ingrid shouted, "Mind you, don't slip!" and went down herself.

Lucy, who was coming along behind, went down simultaneously, her feet shot out from under her and she landed on the softness of the hay net. Their laughter was added to by Alira's face of consternation and anxious whinnying, partly because her owners were both on the floor but mostly because of the resulting delay in her breakfast arriving!

Whilst they quickly tied her up to eat hay while they mucked out, they discussed what to do. They could not at present take her out to the field without risking her falling on the ice but she was full of energy. Their conversation was halted by the appearance of Liz.

"No turnout today" she said abruptly.

Lucy had to take courage into her hands and ask if there was any chance of some rock salt, to improve the yard? The answer was blown away with the rising wind, which seemed to be bringing more snow, and Liz hurried away, no doubt to struggle with attending to her own horses.

"What are we going to do with her?" Ingrid voiced the sentiment for both of them as Lucy took her rugs off.

She was fit, blooming muscles evident beneath her shiny coat, excited to see what was going to happen next. Ingrid was adamant that she could not just stay in her stable, she would become demented without exercise and all hell would break loose when she could finally be led out.

"Perhaps we can dig out a track round the yard and put some grit down so she doesn't slip, then walk her out in hand tonight? Then maybe the snow will go tomorrow!"

Lucy looked doubtful but hoped Ingrid was right. They got busy feeding her, mucking out, grooming her, picking her feet out, changing her rugs and adding an extra one, then the hardest bit: digging a path to the muck-heap through the thick snow, wrestling the barrow down to it and back, making the yard ascent to get shavings from the barn, descending the yard with the barrow this time, bags of shavings balanced precariously on the top. They gave their mare a decent bed and then left to make the difficult journey home again, thankfully mostly downhill this time. They were both sweating beneath the insulating layers of clothing they had put on and very aware of time ticking away; when they rang their places of work to explain the delay and the amount of snow in the countryside, their employers were understanding. The North/South motorway was closed due to heavy snow and stranded vehicles, the minor roads were known to be treacherous, so it seemed that after all this they may not get to work anyway!

That night, an excited Alira was introduced to a snowy world that inhibited her desire to fly about; she was led around the track which had been dug out mostly by Ingrid; she looked like a racehorse in the paddock before the Derby, her neck arched, champing her bit and stepping out with alacrity.

How much walking would it take for this horse to be exercised? Lucy wondered.

But slowly she did relax, dropped her head, stretched out her frame and rhythmically swung into her stride, enjoying the movement and matching her leader's speed, or was it that Lucy matched her speed? Lucy certainly knew that it was her maximum stride and she was perspiring as she walked around and around and then changed the rein to do the same on the opposite circle. Eventually, she returned the mare to the box, which Ingrid had made ready for her. "Good girl, good girl" Lucy was delighted that it had gone well and Alira seemed calm now.

But the snow did not go by the next day, nor the next nor the day after that. The thick white blanket that enveloped the land stayed for three weeks, getting thicker and reaching a depth of three feet up at Ainsty. Nights of freezing temperatures meant it was hazardous to get to the few major roads which were open and Lucy and Ingrid were missing work or being late to work, which caused them a lot of anxiety, but mostly they were concerned about the little horse, who was jumping out of her skin in the stable up at Ainsty.

Other people's horses seemed content to chew hay and wait in their stables until the snow had gone. But Alira was circuiting her box, chewing wood, was desperate to use up some of her energy and the only way they could do it was to walk her round the yard, twice a day, after putting down salted grit to stop the risk of slipping. Some horses were being taken out onto the area that had grass underneath, by the stud farm sign and they dug down to find some grass to eat; Lucy tried with Alira and found the horse had no idea what to do. When Lucy did not let her go anywhere, she did paw the ground with impatience and therefore move some snow but did not keep at it in the same place and even when she did manage to expose some grass with Lucy's help, snuffled at it and disregarded it, nasty cold stuff she thought!

After a week of this, Ingrid suggested that they try lunging her in the ménage in the snow, because she was capering around whilst being led, trying to escape and amusing herself by prancing and bucking. The Saturday morning, that they tried this was captured on film, which made hilarious viewing, for she tried to gallop and bound through the snow like dogs do, very happy and excited but a bit wild as well. Not very orthodox.

Another week passed and the drive between the trees which led down to Liz's stables had been cleared by a tractor and Liz said they could use the lunge pen by her stables to exercise her. The two of them took her with a rein on the bridle at the off side and the lunge line on the other side and managed to get her safely over the ruts and chunks of ice and snow, well booted up as she was. Once in the lunge pen with Lucy in the centre and Ingrid watching through the gate her pent-up energy was too much for her to listen to commands or signals from the whip or lunge line, she raced round leaping and bucking, gaining far too much speed and came down, her legs straight out from under her. She was up as sharp as a shot, but it did slow her down temporarily, although maintaining a walk or trot seemed to be too much to ask and soon she was cantering again and they thought it best to call a halt to the excitement. The walk back up to the stable was entertaining, as she was even more fired up now, but once back in the stable she relaxed. She had sustained a strain in the muscle above her hock, but another few days of walking put it right, although Alira found this unreasonably boring, however much they tried to vary it.

One dark night. Lucy walked her into the ménage; there were lights that shone over there but they still left pools of blackness that made a horse spooky. The snow in there had now become compacted and due to a severe frost was hard and slippery. However, some grass was exposed on the far bank so Lucy led her carefully across to let her eat, which Alira did with gusto this time, Lucy standing quietly beside her. Suddenly, Alira whipped round like a shot, startled by a shadow or something, unfortunately turning towards the side where Lucy was standing and flattening Lucy onto the ice.

Lucy had such a shock, as all her breath was knocked out of her she saw hooves above her face but none hit her. As she recovered, she felt too winded to get up but turned her head to see where her horse had gone and was relieved to see her standing by her stables, looking uneasy with her lead rope trailing. Lucy got stiffly to her feet and went across to Alira, but the mare was unnerved and shied away; Ingrid now came to see where they had gone and helped to catch the naughty horse. They were to always have this problem, that their mare never really respected a person's space, if she was upset, excited, frightened or furious she forgot all about people on the ground and went right through them. Lucy's aching bones ached more than usual for a good while and she told herself for the hundredth time not to take risks, but the fact was she would do anything she physically could for this horse and that drove her on to display strength and fortitude in the face of physical pain and some weakness.

The snow did at last come to an end and water ran everywhere, the earth seemed to be singing with joy as little babbling brooks arose and led the water away from the land. With the thawing of the snow came permission to turn the horses out again, back again to the lower field where the snow had thawed more quickly and some grass could be had.

Lucy thought, *Oh, my God! I have to get her there!* for it was her turn to do morning stables that day. A change in the endless walking around the yard, but how excited was Alira going to be during the walk through the trees? All that pent-up energy was going to take some holding in, but Lucy set out with her charge cheerfully enough.

Up through the yard, the mare alert, stepping out with her big, rhythmic walk. Onto the tarmac of the lane where her feet made clattering, echoing music as her excitement grew and her 15.2 hands high seemed to become 16.2 hands high. The neck beside Lucy hardened as the muscles tensed and energy pulsed through the mare's system, her ears now so pricked that they seemed to meet at the tips, her eyes were bright, her mouth short, but the top lip was protruding like a foal's mouth. Alira wanted to go! Turning down the avenue beneath the trees, it seemed as if her feet were all above the ground and her shoulder was pushing Lucy into the trees, she spun round and tried to take off, but Lucy battled manfully not to let her go – who knew when she would stop? No time soon, of that she was sure.

Now Alira was plunging and cantering sideways and that big muscular shoulder was too strong to defy. Lucy found herself among the trees with her, brambles snagging, tree stumps tripping, she was losing her… but then managed to wind the rope around a narrow tree that could hold her firmly. Alira was furious, fighting, cantering on the spot, shaking her head to free the rope. Lucy let her use up some energy then took the rope very firmly near the bit, they were half way there; she just had to get her to that gate!

Champing the bit and proving that one day she would be very capable of piaffe, Alira pranced beside her; at last, here was the gate and she got her through. Unfastened the bridle, swung her round, she flew back against the bridle which slipped from her head and enabled her to launch herself forward and away like a cannon ball unleashed. Heedless of the wet ground, all that power thrust her into a headlong gallop, hooves thundering and splashing across the field.

Then she leaped into the air, she was loving her freedom; next bucked and kicked, galloped on then skidded onto her haunches to rear into the air, standing on her hind legs then off again to race in her head with another hundred horses. Even though, in reality, the other mares were standing watching, closely grouped, alarmed; Onyx occasionally trotted a tight circle around them, head high, but they were confused, perplexed by such energy when they could perceive no threat, the galloping horse displayed such enthusiasm, but was such a liability, mostly to herself.

The land had become muddy and slippery, treacherous for galloping horses, who in turn ploughed it with their deep muddy hoofmarks, or at least Alira did, enraging Liz, who had to move the group of mares again, for Alira did so much damage with her wild gallop before she took up her position in the gateway. Liz having decreed that they should go back into the long field of previous occupancy, the mare did stop her gate habit and grazed with the group again. When she had had her fling, which now seemed to end with a skid onto her haunches, digging her hind feet in, wreaking more destruction on the field and who knows what level of strain to her legs.

Chapter 11
Alira Goes Missing

Temperatures rose a little, but rain became the order of each day and one dark, overcast day they had further problems. Lucy was going to be the one to get her in as she was the earliest to finish work, but traffic was building up on all the roads that led her towards Ainsty; it was already dark when she got there, the sky overcast so no moon to reveal even an inkling of light in the sky. Telling herself to keep calm, that Alira would be fine, Lucy hurried to the field. When she got to the field, nothing was fine at all; there was no sign of Alira! She hurriedly ran back up to the yard to see if someone else had got her in, but no, the other mares were in, but nobody had seen Alira, they had not thought that she was still out there. Running back down to the field with beating heart, Lucy phoned her home as she patrolled the field. James and Sophie were on their way to help. But what could they do? The horse was missing, gone.

Lucy went up and down the field in the dark, calling her horse, combing every inch of the rough hillocky acres, to no avail. She must be stolen; there was access to the estate by a track that ran on further down through the trees and travellers camped there. They could have seen the speed of her gallop and come to get her for illicit racing or just to sell, or maybe she had got out somehow and galloped away to who knew what fate? Perhaps disorientated by the dark, she could not find her way back to the stables and then something had frightened her. Lucy's mind ran on and on, it was all her fault, she should have rung someone to go and get Alira, but nobody would want to and it was always a risk that the mare would knock them for six or stamp on their foot or something.

Tears pricked at the back of Lucy's eyes; how could anyone lose a whole horse? Was this to be the end of it all, just nothing, the big brown animal nowhere to be seen, a void in their lives where there was such challenge and excitement?

Time passed, the darkness deepened, the cold got worse and now the rest of the people on the yard realised a situation was evolving that had dire implications. Onyx's owner, who until now had not been particularly friendly, was full of concern and drove her car down to the field to shine the headlights across it. Tom materialised to rattle a bucket of feed to see if she would come, James and Sophie arrived to find a distraught Lucy, shivering with a chill that went right through her. Sophie went into the field to walk the fence lines and soon after there was a shout from her – Lucy raced in her direction, expecting she had found an ill or dead horse on the ground, for surely that was the only way she could have missed her?

Car headlights enabled a shadowy image to be revealed, Sophie holding a rearing animal, a horse who was spinning round her, crazy with whites of her eyes showing – Alira!

"Hold on!" shouted Lucy.

Sophie did, with all her might, for the mare was very upset and frightened. Lucy went and got hold of her, only to be almost dragged off her feet as Alira tried to bolt away. The only way she got her to the gate was to wrestle her across to the fence then led her with one elbow into the base of her neck, her head pulled round and utilising a strength she could find now, born of adrenaline and single-minded determination.

Sophie was now busy telling Ingrid, who had appeared looking stricken, not sure what was going on, how she had decided to walk the perimeter of the field, looking for any gap in the fence where Alira might have escaped. She had come across Alira packed tightly with her hindquarters into the corner, reversed as far back as she could into the thick hedge, almost enveloped with the branches, rigid and shrunken into herself, obviously too terrified to move and Sophie could only coax her out with much encouragement, after which the horse panicked and tried to get free. She was clearly terrified of the dark and had tried to hide herself, only to cause mayhem with everyone trying to find her. Horses are not normally afraid of the dark, but this one was and now as Lucy wrestled her way back to the gate with the snorting horse. Alira was blinded by headlights and getting more and more upset. A shout from Lucy got them to turn off the car headlights before she lost the horse again into the engulfing darkness.

With great relief, she handed her to Ingrid, who led her without incident back to the yard and everyone gradually returned to their evening stable duties or went away home. The well-lit familiarity of the yard at last relaxed Alira and she was given a warm feed and rugged up well in a deep, clean bed of shavings.

"Oh God! I'm so relieved!" gasped Lucy and her daughter agreed, "What a nightmare!"

Then they laughed at the unintended pun, tension relieving itself and making it seem hilarious.

Later, Lucy and Ingrid sat down with James and Sophie to drink tea and eat some food – they realised they faced a difficult problem; if she was unable to stay out in the dark and it was dark every night by the time they returned from work, what could they do? She needed to go out to prevent her going stir-crazy in the stable all day, yet soon it would be dark in the mornings too. They had to ask for help; they had no confidence that it would be forthcoming, but there seemed no other option.

Ultimately, it was Liz who made the offer; for a couple of extra quid each day she would turn her out and bring her in after two or three hours. Nobody else fancied the daunting job of leading Alira about and most people were busy with their own horses, but Liz was always there and not afraid of an excitable horse.

This arrangement worked okay although Alira's owners suffered anxiety wondering if their horse would be all right. Well, she was, after her mad fling around the field she would wait to come in, by the gate. She was a 'gate horse' and the pile of dung was testament to the fact that she had been stood there all the time, when Liz went to get her. Liz knew a great deal about horses but did not have any explanation as to why this one behaved in such an inexplicable way. What she did know was that a great deal of damage was being caused to her field by the galloping; this one didn't seem bothered about grass but Liz had other horses to think about and they needed it! The wet weather continued and the hoofmarks in the mares' field were readily apparent; hoofmarks, skid marks and deep holes where she had been bucking.

Ingrid was getting ready to ride her one Saturday morning when Liz addressed her. "Your mare has made a right mess of that field! There's marks everywhere, it's no good, she can't go out if she's doing that! She's ploughing it!"

Ingrid apologised but pointed out how long the horses had been kept in by the snow, tried to say that she was sure Alira would settle down, although her words lacked conviction, even to herself.

"Work!" replied Liz, "She needs more work to quieten her down. Take her for a gallop in the stubble field."

She tramped away, leaving Ingrid to wonder how any amount of work would stop the galloping, somehow when this Oldenburg had been born there were too few genes from the old, heavy horses and too many of the Thoroughbred genes which had lightened the breed.

Ingrid was back in the stable now and gazed at her lovely mare, grateful for the sturdy legs with eight inches of bone that just might survive all the stress put on them when she treated the field like a racetrack. She wondered how the little horse had that pretty, dished face and wide cheekbones, more reminiscent of an Arab horse than the slightly Roman-nosed Oldenburg breed.

Distressed that her horse seemed to be antagonising people again, she led the enthusiastic animal up to the ménage to mount and commence her ten minutes walking to warm her up. Sometimes, this felt somewhat precarious, because the mare's back would be up and Ingrid was aware of the little power pack of energy beneath her, not quite certain what she might do.

Concerns about cases at work were going through her head, children and parents who demanded, not surprisingly, an immense input from her to deal with their special needs. But these thoughts were banished as soon as she asked Alira to trot on, for she would always spring into trot with alacrity, grabbing the bit and trying to take control. It took all her rider's concentration to keep control and steer her into the shapes she required, to keep her safe, keep her supple, keep her in a rhythmic pace which was not rushing but still allowed her to use herself for she was all about movement, loving to stretch her legs and show off her scope. But Ingrid could get her to settle into an obedient working trot that was lovely to watch. In fact, some of the other liveries would sometimes appear, even on wet and cold, dark nights, to watch her work the little mare, changing the rein, settling her down, enlarging the circle, using the circumference of the school, then bringing her in to bend her around her inside leg, always patient, always firmly ensuring compliance.

The visual effect was one of ease and harmony, but sometimes Ingrid was battling a very strong horse, who was leaning on the bit and difficult to turn. When canter was introduced into the session, it was with high-blown snorting and much champing of the bit as the mare fought to take control and set her jaw against the bit, leaving Ingrid in a situation akin to driving a fast car with no steering or brakes. The schooling area was small and Ingrid imagined the pair of them sailing off the edge down the precipitous bank to the field below, taking the fence with them and not surviving unscathed. It did not happen, but she had to ride every stride to keep the impression of a future dressage horse being schooled, rather than a green youngster dictating the pace to her rider.

Ingrid took on board to an extent, the words that Liz had spoken and tried to ride her every day and even take her out hacking on the weekend – the nights were still too dark to allow it to happen during the week. Ingrid would walk her down the estate road, every step a hesitation, the young mare's eyes on stalks, head held high, muscles hard and her owner reassuring her all the time with legs closed around her, gentle contact on the bit, soothing words and frequent pats on the neck.

The fairly short distance would take a long time and Alira would be tired upon return. "Liz must be joking if she thinks I am taking her up onto the plough!" Ingrid confided to Lucy. "I would lose her altogether if she galloped and it would wreak havoc with her legs! I want her for dressage, not hunting! The surface is all mud and stones and she would be freaked out by the open space and just bolt."

Lucy was in agreement that nothing would be gained by galloping her, but she thought that plenty of steady trotting on roads and tracks was a good way to get her to use up some energy. One day, Lucy could not resist a ride on her, not wanting to expect something of her daughter she was not prepared to do herself.

The particular Saturday morning that Lucy got onto Alira's broad back was a dismal, damp February day, with mist and fog swirling around the trees, drips hanging off the branches and a muted atmosphere where the usual birdsong was unheard. Lucy felt considerably thrilled to be sitting on her own horse and picked up the reins as if she had been riding every day, some muscle memory enabling her to sit just as elegantly as she had ever sat, carefully talking to the mare to ensure that she knew it was the person she knew so well.

They set off out of the yard with the horse looking eagerly ahead, turned towards the gate of the estate, a mile or so away up the long drive through the trees. She urged her into a trot and felt the powerful swinging gait, realising that she did not have the strength in her legs that she used to have, but finding the rhythm of the trot and keeping Alira focused as they trotted past the field where the geldings were alert to the mare that was moving quickly past them. Lucy's heart sang as she felt the old joy in the freedom, the movement, the excitement of being at one with her horse, a creature which it seemed she was akin to, fascinated by and forever in admiration of. She felt the power in this animal, a union with her, exhilaration and pride. There was nowhere on this earth she would rather be.

All was well until the mare suddenly panicked when they reached the end of the drive. She shied violently, half reared, spun around and started snorting in horror at a contingent of men carrying guns and followed by dogs, who were coming out of the area behind the gatehouse where Liz and her gamekeeper husband lived. Alira was petrified for some reason and prepared to bolt home; Lucy could only think how much more her body would hurt if she had a riding accident, so slipped off her back and led her into the tree-lined space to the side of Liz's house. Once the mare had registered where she was and what was happening, Alira calmed down and Lucy asked one of the shooting men for a leg-up, so she was back on board and feeling confident again. Then in the way that would always happen with Lucy and Alira, the unexpected and bizarre happened, just to add to the difficulty of containing this volatile horse.

The shooters decided to push out a sort of cabin on wheels, covered in camouflage net and moving silently it came out of the trees, several men partially hidden behind it so it appeared to have legs as well as wheels.

Oh no! That snort, which Lucy now knew meant a panic attack in the mare, and she was off down the road. Lucy wrestled to turn her without making her slip, it was as if the horse had no mouth to respond to the bit, no hearing for the words of 'Whoa girl, whoa girl' that Lucy said in vain. Lucy thought that hopefully they could get away from the beastly thing as they continued back down the road, bounding and circling with the horse fighting for her head, then Lucy realised that the 'monster' was continuing to pursue them as the men pushed the hut down the road! Probably it was to be used as a hide where they could sit among the trees and keep dry while they waited for the dogs and beaters to drive the pheasants towards them.

Lucy's strength was failing now. She had not ridden for years and her arms and legs were shaking with the effort of trying to stop Alira from bolting, whilst staying on top. At one point, the horse slightly got her head and tried to gallop down the road, Lucy desperately pulled her into the trees and she crashed through the undergrowth, her rider dipping low to avoid branches and then she stopped. They had come across some high wire mesh deer fencing that blocked any exit from the estate in this direction.

This saved Lucy from losing control and returning to the yard on a bolting horse who no doubt would have fallen as she made the turn into the yard, instead she slipped from the mare's back and grabbed her head in order to lead her home. This would be no easy task, for her horse was wired and when they emerged from the trees Lucy expostulated. "That bloody thing is still coming!" And Alira, although further away from it now, was prancing with head held high, whites of her eyes showing as she struggled to see the monster behind her and her hooves were dancing on the tarmac.

Grimly, Lucy twisted the bit in her mouth and once again resolved not to let go, somehow managing to contain her until they turned into the yard, Ingrid somewhat alarmed to see her mother leading the horse now and the animal dark with sweat and flecked with foam from the bit. The story was relayed and they had to laugh, for if you had designed something to scare the hell out of Alira, this would have been it! She was not afraid once she could understand, but a mechanical object that moved without a sound and had legs too was beyond her comprehension and she never did settle on shooting days after that. Gunshots had always alarmed her and no habituation ever occurred, even though shooting days were a regular occurrence on the Ainsty Estate.

The consequences of the ride for Lucy were dire; it had irritated the arthritic inflammation in her neck and the following day she was dizzy, nauseous and painful, with the acute neck pain eventually leading to a migraine. However, Alira may have benefitted from the experience in some way, because she seemed bolder when Ingrid hacked her out, she had not, after all, been eaten by the monster, nor had she got away with bolting home.

She was being better out hacking, enough for Ingrid to agree to ride with Elaine on Monty and another woman who had one of the geldings, a great big bay. That such a big horse should have such a small rider seemed incongruous; Lindsay was petite, blonde and very pretty, she wore lots of make-up and had all the latest riding gear; she sat atop her tall powerful horse without looking as if she could really control him. Other people had said to Ingrid that the big horse behaved like a stallion around mares, so you had to watch out for him; he was tall but also broad, powerful enough to carry a man let alone Lindsay. But she seemed to manage and Ingrid set out to ride with them one Sunday morning, Lucy full of pride, watching them leave the yard with a clatter of hooves on the tarmac, Ingrid with a few butterflies in her stomach, partly excited, slightly nervous. Her mare was keen to go but receptive to her aids, her neck was arched and she was happy to be in company, braver.

That morning was bright for a January day, a mostly blue sky after a cold night. Some grey clouds were being chased away by a slight breeze, watery sunlight brightening the brown earth, smudged grass and stark trees. A buzzard circled lazily, sadly calling its melancholy cry as it searched for any rabbit heedless enough to venture out onto the sparse grass.

The trio went up the drive, trotted past the gatehouse and so onto the open road. Alira was good with traffic and even undeterred by tractors after her exposure to their noise and smell in her stable at the Equestrian Centre. The string of three horses, all dark bay in colour, soon turned off the road onto a broad swathe of track that led uphill through a plantation.

Here they could ride beside each other and Alira's scopey stride enabled her to stay alongside Prince, the big bay, while Monty had to jog to keep pace. They walked up the hill then as a vista of planted trees divided by tracks spread before them, went into canter and flew along the track, wind in their faces, deafened by that and the thunder of hooves, splashing through the occasional puddle. Thrilled by motion and movement, each perched on their horse, holding the reins tight but allowing that fluid urgent rhythm to propel them on without a care in the world.

Ingrid's heart sang as Alira powered forwards, Ingrid at first cautious about giving her the reins, but then 'Go girl!' and all she could see was the two pricked ears before her, the rise and fall of mane, the green swathe of grass vanishing beneath her horse's feet. Prince was up alongside, as was Monty, but the two bigger horses drew ahead and left Monty behind as the gradient asked more of them.

Now Lindsay shouted, "We need to turn left here!"

And they were all slowing down, sitting down in their saddles to bring the horses' heads back and gradually return to trot, turning slightly then at right angles through another, narrower path through the trees.

Suddenly, a deer jumped out, right in front of Alira, vanishing quickly after darting across the path; the mare hardly hesitated, to Ingrid's surprise, she just trotted right on. Soon they had another canter, then trotted on through endless conifers, now turning downhill again towards home, coming steadily back to walk and chance to chat as they headed on down the hill.

Ingrid was thrilled with her mare, her good behaviour, hardly a shy, willingness to go exactly where she told her to go and then the control she had in canter, no attempt to gallop and an easy ability to bring her back to trot. When they finally rode back into the stable yard, their hooves rattling the old buildings from their sleep, Ingrid jumped off and led her to find Lucy, who had been busy cleaning up the tack room while she waited for her daughter's return.

"Has she been any trouble?" she called, seeing the outline of a horse in the doorway.

"Not at all! She's been brilliant!" enthused Ingrid and went on to tell her all the details while she untacked and Lucy rubbed the horse down.

They both went home happy, hungry for a late lunch, keen to plan the agenda for their horse the following week. They were getting increasingly frustrated with having only the small area at Ainsty to school in and Ingrid was finding it difficult to get Alira to concentrate in the dark when there were just two floodlights and many dark shadows. Circling was constrained by the surface falling away at the edges, dangerous for a hoof to be lost over. And when the weather was bad it was grim, trying to deal with these difficulties and contend with an excited horse in the wind or a reluctant horse in the rain and on top of all that, Ingrid was keen to compete soon so they needed a mode of transport!

Lucy remembered the words of the man who, upon being told they had bought a horse, had said, "Well, that is the cheapest thing you will ever do now."

He was right, for along with livery bills, feed and bedding, they had insured their special horse and now were contemplating buying a trailer! When they got it, the challenge was to make Alira go in it, and Lucy spent many hours, initially getting her to stand on the ramp, then getting her to walk through, round again and through, but struggled to get her to stand quietly inside the trailer. Also, there were days when she just would not go in. There are few things more frustrating than planning to go somewhere with a horse and it refuses to load.

Liz had come across them trying to get Alira in one day and quickly decided to help them by grabbing a yard broom and shoving it under Alira's tail. The horse bounded forwards, almost landing on Lucy who was at her head, then when Liz re-applied the broom, reared and still refused to go into the trailer, now getting herself agitated and furious, stubborn as a mule and strong as an ox.

That day they never did get her in, but there were days when she went in and they took her for a short ride to familiarise her with the motion and the inevitable hills which they had to go negotiate. Alira would shriek and whinny all the way, telling them that she was there, sometimes banging the trailer until it frightened sheep in the fields and kids on bikes, who no doubt wondered if there was a wild stallion in there.

Progress was being made! There were lots more things that they could do with their horse than when they came to Ainsty Stud and she was a lot more obliging in the stable, whilst being schooled and out hacking. Ingrid was feeling a rapport with her young horse and trust was starting to grow between them.

Life with Alira Compliquer never ran smoothly. They should have known that something would come along to cause hiatus.

Chapter 12
Disaster Strikes

After hacking out with Prince and Monty, Ingrid, Elaine and Lindsay agreed that they would go again the following weekend. So on a Saturday morning that dawned mild, almost spring-like, the three women emerged into a quiet stable yard carrying saddles and bridles, having groomed their horses.

The stable yard was tranquil; a pair of doves cooing to each other in anticipation of nesting, but a certain cold dampness hung in the air. Soon the yard seemed lively. Monty was standing obediently waiting with pricked ears, Prince seemed to fill the yard because of his size, but so did Alira, because of her charisma and presence. The big gelding stood with his ears back, stamping and swishing his tail. Alira danced in expectation of exercise; Lucy held the offside stirrup while Ingrid got on.

"Have a good ride," she beamed, delighted.

This was why she wanted Ingrid to have a horse: to have fun and fresh air, to enjoy riding and enjoy the companionship of her horse, as well as the company of other people who also loved horses. Lucy watched as they rode out of the yard, picking up their reins and setting off in the same direction, Alira shining like a star with the bloom on her coat, the shine of her eyes as she carried Ingrid with pride and dignity, on her toes, but obedient.

Initially, Ingrid felt the mare's back was up and so was slightly anxious, but then as they broke into trot, setting off in the same direction, the mare put her little head down and was purposeful. Ingrid relaxed; she knew Alira was happy and intent on her job. Lucy was watching from the stone wheel that announced 'Ainsty Stud' and felt happy for her horse and her daughter.

Then suddenly, Lucy could hardly believe her eyes as the three horses skittered apart and Alira was rearing! She had run back to where the edge of the road fell away and was high in the air, vertical, a full rear and faltering on the very edge of the road, pawing the air as if desperately trying to get down again but could not. Ingrid was leaning as far forwards as she possibly could, leaning down beside the mare's neck, doing everything she could to bring her down from her perilous position.

Lucy's heart was racing as she ran up the road, not knowing what was wrong with Alira, yelling, "Get off her! Get off!" thinking the horse had gone mad and was going to go over backwards and crush Ingrid, possibly break her own back.

Now Alira came down onto her forelegs and her head dropped. She swayed as Ingrid half fell off, half dismounted, bringing the stirrup leather with her. Lucy saw that she was all right although ashen, grabbed the mare's bridle to get her away from the other horses and turn her back towards home. That was when she saw it.

Blood pouring down Alira's head, coming from her eye, then saw her offside eye, almost out of its socket, a hideous mess of crushed eyeball and blood.

"Call the vet, right now, it's an emergency!"

Ingrid was right behind and was on her mobile phone straightaway, catching up with Lucy as she led the disorientated horse back towards the yard, unaware as yet of the mess at the other side of the horse's head.

"Prince kicked her, he suddenly lashed out, he has big shoes on and she reeled and stood right up. I think she was nearly knocked out or in awful pain, she wasn't being naughty, I thought she would go over backwards – oh hello!" – as the veterinary surgery answered, she gasped, for Lucy had turned Alira's head, "We need you to come to Ainsty Stud, Alira has had an awful kick."

Then they were coaxing and soothing the mare, getting her back to the stable and trying not to cry, their beautiful horse, so hurt and so disfigured, it was like a bad dream, a literal nightmare, how had it happened so suddenly and without warning? Hateful great horse; Lucy cursed the animal and Ingrid felt so bad that her little mare had been being so good, did nothing to cause a problem, when out of the blue the big gelding had decided to try and kick her horse's brains out. He had been known to behave like a stallion, so maybe the fact that Alira was coming up alongside triggered some instinct to get her back into her place behind him, but he had never minded the other day!

These whirling thoughts had to be put aside, for they were back in the stable now and making every effort to make Alira comfortable, taking her saddle off, undoing the bridle to get it off her head without touching the wounded eye. The mare was sweating with pain and shock, rocking as her big heart pounded, her head still low and blood dripping down. Lucy kept her as still as possible while Ingrid fetched cotton wool and saltwater to start cleaning away some blood. Then the vet arrived and gave Alira a jab of ketamine to calm her and dull the pain. Lucy felt the heartbeats slow down as the drug took effect, nursed the horse's head against her as the vet examined the injured eye, looking concerned.

Lucy held the immense weight of Alira's head and hardly dared to ask, "Will she be able to see?"

"Well, she cannot now," came the vet's reply, "It is too soon to say whether we can save her sight in that eye."

Lucy and Ingrid were very quiet, each with a lump in their chest. "I can't believe it, it's too awful," said Ingrid.

Lucy's mother instinct diminished her own distress as she tried to say it might be okay, even though looking at the eye she did not feel confident. That they had arrived at such an impasse so soon was so disappointing, but she was also aware that things could have been much, much worse; if Alira had tipped over backwards down that verge, Ingrid could have been very badly injured and it might have been the end of their horse.

"Her offside eye is damaged, badly cut above and below," the vet explained. "There is a nail hole from the other horse's shoe above the inner corner and severe swelling. It has stopped bleeding now but the aqueous humour is the liquid that you can see escaping."

His objective assessment belied the emotions that his words invoked: poor, poor Alira! She did not deserve this! They felt so sorry for her, her usual sparkle dulled by the experience and the tranquiliser and now the injections, of anti-inflammatory and antibiotics. The vet put spray on cuts on her hind legs. She had also scraped the skin off her nearside hock and cut the inside of her near hind from hock to fetlock, not deeply but as a result of standing on herself, for her brushing boot had come down over her hoof. She was going to be a nursing case for quite a while.

More time in the stable. Twice daily bathing the eye with salt water and she was such a good girl! Since the accident, she seemed to have understood more than ever that these were her people, they cared for her and she tolerated their medical and healing procedures really well. She was quite subdued and sorry for herself for a few days, probably had concussion, plus her world was disorienting, seeing out of only one eye.

Ingrid and Lucy were also subdued and both found that the accident replayed visually in their heads, over and over again, yet all they wanted to do was forget it. Lucy had to go through it verbally with the insurers and thankfully, they were paying the vet bills, after the excess. They could not sue Lindsay because she was not insured and much as they were angry about her horse being so violent, it is one of those things, one of those risks, accidents that can occur between powerful, unpredictable animals. Lindsay and Elaine both tiptoed around Alira's two owners, more so because it seemed that Prince had harmed other horses before, but nobody had warned them of this side of his nature. Elaine doggedly insisted on saying that she did not see anything happen at all, when she must have done, being right up alongside.

People appeared to take a peek at the state of the newest, most beautiful horse's face, all damaged and bloody. Even Tom came, asking in his broad Yorkshire accent, "Has your pony had a poke in 't eye then?"

Afterwards, they had to laugh, his dry Yorkshire outlook minimised their experience and their horse so much! Nobody was allowed to fuss with Alira, nor did they want to, for the risk at this stage was infection. With no riding for them to undertake, Lucy and Ingrid used their energy to keep everything scrupulously clean and did everything they could to keep her comfortable and calm – if she were to knock that eye or rub it, it would be awful. Lucy could remember once seeing a half blind dressage horse, it just had a hole where the eye should have been at one side of its head; it did compete but had no flair or presence and she could not recall it ever being placed. A dark time for both of them and difficult not to feel angry about something like this happening, just as Alira was getting going under saddle.

There were several visits from the veterinary practise and the vets were impressed with the improvement of the injury and the care it was receiving. Some five days after the kick had happened, the vet carefully examined the eye and imparted the joyous news that he thought yes, Alira would keep her sight!

Her owners' relief was tremendous and some dark shadows cleared. They could now take her out of the stable too, an experience which Alira was very nervous about, but was reasonably well behaved. She could not see clearly yet so lots of things spooked her, but she enjoyed stretching her legs. What was more, she seemed sound and not to have any other serious results of the kick in the head which must have caused her extreme pain and nearly knocked her unconscious. Her energy returned and they lunged her, led her in the yard in hand, noting how she was nervous if another horse passed her, this needed working on. Eventually, Ingrid rode her again, finding to her shock and surprise that it was not just the horse that was hesitant. She felt nervous and anxious in the saddle, had lost some of her confidence and needed to just work her mare quietly by herself for a time, to forget the panic that rear had induced and forget the horror of the bloody consequences of the kick. Lucy did what she could to reassure her, but inevitably, she too felt anxious, not wanting Ingrid to risk any negative reactions to her riding of Alira.

Firstly, Ingrid and Alira trotted quietly around the ménage; the mare was a little unbalanced at first, not surprisingly. The swelling of the eye was almost gone, the scab on the inner side of the eye was dry and the other area still needed to heal. Bad weather worked against her continued return to work, for February was to justify its historical name of 'February fill-dyke' and day after day was either wet and windy or misty, drizzly and cold. Not something riders of stabled horses can usually allow to stop them, but they had to keep the eye dry until there was no area of open wound.

The next time Ingrid rode, Alira got very upset about the hunt coming by. The estate was regularly traversed by both foxhounds and beagles, which always got Alira anxious and sweaty, as did the sound of shots when shooting took place. This time, her stress when returned to the stable caused her to injure her leg and she walked out lame the next day. Another week of walking in hand followed, at the end of which she was performing acrobatics, convincing them she needed to be in work again. However, she worked well in the schooling area and Ingrid was pleased to think she had not lost the trust and cooperation of her mount, despite the interruptions that had made her worry that all the work they had done would be to no avail.

Then the following day was windy, although dry; many horses are spooky in the wind but Alira was just wild on this day, filling Ingrid with doubt again. She kept working her every time she could and their work was developing gradually, if hesitantly; Ingrid was asking her to leg yield now to show how she was learning to be responsive to the leg aids quickly and specifically, as well as becoming more supple and aware of how she was moving.

More interruption occurred when she cast a shoe, "But this is the way of it with horses," Lucy said, "Two steps forward, one back if you are lucky enough not to have three steps back!"

Ingrid felt the steps backwards were more apparent when she rode her up to the gatehouse one weekend and felt Alira taut and strained, all her new-found confidence on the road gone. Her back was up and she fell behind the bit, making no contact with her mouth whatsoever, resulting in Ingrid being left without control – if she shortened her reins to the point where she made it impossible for Alira to avoid the bit, the mare's jaw was set and her neck rigid, so her rider was left ineffectual anyway.

The horse's sides, too, were hard and numb to the insistence of Ingrid's legs; where a light pressure caused a response in the ménage, even a kick drew little response now. This made the ride difficult, for when Alira reached the point where Prince had kicked her, she refused to go forward and Ingrid had no aids to make her.

Ultimately, she managed to get the mare past that point, but there were many other hesitations and shies, even in that short distance. Ingrid persevered; the next day got her trotting up there, but with similar difficulty. The following weekends involved variation from schooling by taking her out and around the estate. But the horse felt unreliable, explosive and was trying to bolt for home when anything frightened her, which could be anything from an open space glimpsed through a gateway to a vehicle or just a sound, or indeed nothing explicit to human perception.

Hacking under these circumstances was not a pleasure and took ages too, the mare was so unsure of herself. Elaine agreed to come with them to see if company helped, but if anything, that made Alira worse, she did not find the presence of Monty reassuring.

The culmination of these hacking experiences happened one Saturday when Ingrid rode Alira up towards the gatehouse by herself and a tractor came down the road. Spring was not far away but the sky was full of lowering clouds, stacking up with increasing greyness and filling the air with a frosty coldness, with the possibility that the rain might fall as snow. Alira started napping when they got to the point where she had been kicked by Prince, was reluctant to go forwards, running back, curling herself into a half moon shape so that Ingrid could do nothing with her and the distant, approaching tractor was only adding to their problems. She had not been frightened of tractors previously, but since her accident many things were used by her as an excuse to try and return home, and Ingrid was filled with doom, seeing the huge thing coming while her horse was in this mood.

The estate had a lot of arable land so all the machinery was huge; there would be no room for the tractor to come past unless she could get Alira onto the grass. Alira refused to step onto the grass for no apparent reason other than that she was protesting pretty strongly about going hacking at all. When the tractor came up to them, the driver was considerate and slowed right down, but Alira was still in the middle of the road, spinning round, her hooves scrabbling on the tarmac, now introducing half-rears when Ingrid tried to boot her sides to get her onto the grass.

By now, the tractor had been forced to stop and he even cut his engine to help the rider of the recalcitrant horse. Ingrid got her almost past when Alira ran back into the tractor, oblivious to hurting herself or her rider, up against the great solid wheel, then shot sideways as if electrocuted. The engine roared into life and the tractor departed, for Ingrid and Alira had finally got onto the grass, where now she half-reared every time Ingrid asked her to move at all and threatened to go higher if forced to continue. Ingrid turned back to the stable yard, still fighting her mount, who now wanted to return much faster than Ingrid would have liked! Privately, Ingrid vowed that she was not taking this horse hacking again; she was dangerously unreliable and she found no pleasure in these battles. Her strength was in dressage, that was what Ingrid loved to do and where Alira showed the potential to excel.

Eventually, they could turn Alira out in the field again, for the eye was healing well and the mare was bored with being stabled. Her experience of pain and injury had done nothing to erase the necessity to gallop in the field. She did her customary pocket rocket impression then settled to graze, only to be alarmed by something which set her off again, this time taking the other mares with her, the next time they ignored her, tired of galloping, but she was not! Every gallop left deep hoofmarks and then where Alira had abruptly stopped, long skid marks in the mud, not just in one place but all over the field.

The horses, mainly Alira, had made such a mess in the lower field that Liz moved the mares back into the other field and Alira promptly returned to her habit of standing by the gate most of the time, after she had her obligatory gallop. This once again invoked the wrath of Liz who banned Alira from that field, or any field, Liz said she just could not have this damage to the grassland. Lucy and Ingrid appealed to Liz for Alira to be allowed to share a smaller field, near the stable yard, which was used for another little mare who was on full livery because her owners worked away throughout the week.

"Perhaps she won't gallop so much in there," they cajoled "and Lily is old and calm, so she isn't going to gallop with her."

She responded to Lucy's pleas by giving them one last chance to go out in the field with the aged mare which inhabited a small paddock near to the stable yard.

"Surely," Ingrid responded to the news when Lucy told her, "She will settle in there."

No, Alira did not. The paddock was on a slight slope so she found delight in galloping downhill, then using her hind legs to throw her weight back and plough to a halt, ripping up the grass. Lucy went into the field and stomped down every hoof print and slip mark, but they still were apparent to the eagle eye of Liz and she made it known in no uncertain terms, "I will not have that horse doing any more damage, she will have to stay in the stable!"

94

Ingrid was there now and pleaded that Alira would become unmanageable when kept in all the time, she was getting fit now. But Liz was adamant. Ingrid's fears grew about how explosive the horse would be when kept in all the time when she was perfectly healthy and well, bursting with energy. Ingrid knew that her work commitments might not allow her to ride every single night. Lucy struggled to think how they were going to feed Alira enough food to keep her happy, without increasing her abundant energy to an even greater degree. It seemed that everything they did with Alira was fraught with problems; but then Lucy stood watching Ingrid schooling Alira, saw the obedience, the flow and the fluency of her movement and she thought, *The time is right, let's take her to a competition!*

Chapter 13
Debut

Lucy had never polished her so much as she did that morning, every grooming that she did was thorough, but today it was meticulous and much as Alira flinched at heavy brushing, today the soft brush repeatedly circled every inch of her until she was gleaming. Ingrid was patiently plaiting her mane, initially with difficulty because Alira kept moving, but then Alira decided she quite liked having her mane fiddled with and kept relatively still. They both assessed her eye very carefully; there was some scarring and a bit of scar tissue, but it was almost back to normal. The indent in the inside corner would never go but was scarcely noticeable unless somebody was looking for it; the fact that she was dark bay and therefore black around her eyes was lucky, because the injury was not immediately obvious.

There was a breathless excitement between the two women, which they were trying hard to conceal from Alira. Although at present, she had no idea what was happening. Their thoughts were full of uncertainties; would she load to even get her there? Would she freak out when she arrived at a strange place, busy and noisy? Then in the arena, would she be calm and listen to her rider? Or would she be too unnerved to concentrate and look totally green and inexperienced?

This, however, was a red-letter day. The mare loaded with very little fuss, travelled quite well and then upon arriving at the Equestrian Centre stepped out of the trailer to gaze wide-eyed at her surroundings. There were so many horses and ponies she must have thought it was a party! Everything was different and strange so she thought she had better listen to her owners, she never showed the whites of her eye or tried to defy Lucy or Ingrid. They were to reflect on the way home that their horse's eyes had changed since the accident. There was a softer, deeper expression there which suggested trust and friendliness. In turn, this made her whole face more welcoming and expressive, open to be persuaded to do things and experience changes. Into the warm-up they went, Lucy to the gallery at the side of the arena, pleased to see that Alira was working alongside other horses without fear. Just once, she backed off when a big bay horse tried to disorientate them by coming too close. Soon she was called into the main arena and did a lovely test, neat but fluid, relaxed but obedient. Ingrid was thrilled that she could demonstrate the basic training that she had done, feeling immense satisfaction as the mare responded to her aids.

Lucy walked the mare around the yard of the Equestrian Centre to cool her and calm her, feeling immensely proud of their super horse. All the training was working: hours spent schooling, trailer training, some light hacking, although she would not relax about that since Prince had kicked her – but today she was a dressage horse, had done a Preliminary competition and shown excellent behaviour and great promise – that is what Ingrid wanted her to do, so they were exultant as they returned to Ainsty Stud.

Returning there, a more sombre mood overtook them, for they were not able to put Alira in the field. The early spring weather was not kind to them, for March came in like a lion, with roaring winds and scudding clouds, sometimes rain whipping through the trees. Several times, Ingrid had to go away on a training course and Lucy was left with the job of dealing with a fit horse lacking sufficient outlet for her energy. Lucy would lunge her and was brave enough to do some lunge work in the field, and because it was Alira, there were complications! The wind became a frenzy on this particular day, a veritable gale that sprung up out of nowhere and met woman and horse as they entered the field, Lucy wrestling with the gate, holding Alira with one hand, then whoosh! The wind hit them as they turned across the field, tearing at Alira's mane and causing Lucy to bend into the gale, all the while holding onto her excited horse.

Letting her go onto a circle, she set off at a gallop, plunging through the rushing air, flying round Lucy, who held onto the loop at the end of the lunge line while her precious horse flew around her in a perfect circle but at a flat-out gallop! The horses behind the wall in the next field got excited and just as Lucy had managed to steady her slightly, they rushed up to the wall and set her off again, her body lowered, her mane and tail streaming, her hooves flying over the grass, reverberating against the solid ground.

Lucy thought, *Oh my God! She is going to pull my arms out, but I will not let go of her!*

She did not and at last, Alira slowed and then did some beautiful work on the lunge; when she was listening, she would respond to voice commands, "Walk, Walk on, Trot steady, Trot on, Canter!" Then "Whoa, Whoa – steady," down through each transition and "Stand!" when she would wait for Lucy to come to her for a deserved pat. She could then change the rein and work her in the other direction, to ensure that she did not favour one side, bend more easily one way than the other or prefer one leg to lead on in canter, always ensuring that if she did strike off on the outside leg she came back to trot to obtain the correct lead.

Lucy loved to watch her move with grace and freedom and walked her back through the trees thrilled to have a horse like her in her hands, to be able to work with her, control her fire and channel that energy into calm and fluent responsiveness. That Alira was so vibrant and alive made Lucy feel that their mare was really well again and ready for anything.

However, not being able to turn her out in a field was not sustainable. Lucy and Ingrid reflected that the stud was an ideal environment for a horse who could make use of the big grass fields and the many opportunities for hacking, but neither of these factors now helped Alira and her only focus being dressage meant she relied on the very small ménage, which by now was inhibiting her progress. The Equestrian Centre they had visited to compete had two indoor schools and an outdoor arena; it was forty minutes' journey for Lucy and further for Ingrid, but Ingrid just now was in limbo, having finished a relationship of four years and so looking for a flat. Alira was such an important part of her life that she was prepared to get a flat near Normanton Equestrian Centre to enable her to look after Alira.

They were on the move again!

Chapter 14
Complicated She Is – Leaving Ainsty

The day they left Ainsty Stud was cold and windy with sudden squalls of rain appearing from nowhere; as they drove away up the long drive signs of spring were definitely appearing, with trees beginning to be green and swathes of bluebells in the woods. French partridges materialised from the verge hurrying to hide in the undergrowth at the other side, red legs fast beneath chubby bodies. Two deer were shadows which disappeared almost before they registered in their consciousness and a stoat flashed himself before them, handsome and busy with his world, a life obscured by caution and his feisty determination to exist whether the gamekeeper wanted him to or not.

Lucy drove carefully, not wanting to upset the nervous beast behind her in the trailer, who was whinnying now to the horses in the fields. Restless trampling occurred as they turned down the steep hill away from Ainsty; hopefully, she was leaning on the breast bar, but she didn't always remember simple things that made her life easier, so was possibly too busy looking out of the window of the trailer to balance herself!

"I am sad to leave there in some ways, it has been her first proper livery stable, we've been there for months, but in other ways, I have had enough of cattle! And not being able to turn her out is so frustrating!" Ingrid reflected.

"I know," agreed Lucy, "It is a beautiful place, but kind of sad, especially since Liz's son died."

They had both been to the funeral, Liz's son only in his late twenties, had been killed in Afghanistan, a serving soldier, victim of a roadside bomb. Lucy thought that it must be impossible to survive the loss of a child, grown into an adult but departing this earth before you, his parent, who could not be a guardian when the young man decided to live a life of risk.

Shaking off a sudden feeling of melancholy, Lucy drove with more purpose and intent, seeming to then focus Alira's mind on standing square, legs slightly splayed to achieve balance on a moving floor. They could only assume that she was stood like this, because of course, you cannot see into a trailer from the vehicle.

They were now making it into more civilised lands, down country; less hilly and composed more of grassland farms. Through quite a few small villages, making Lucy muse that she was likely to become very familiar with this journey, now their horse was to be living down here. Soon, they rumbled down a long drive that led to the Equestrian Centre, arable fields at each side of them, giving way to grass fields again as they grew closer. One field had a herd of horses who were at livery here, but these were not to be colleagues of Alira. Lucy and Ingrid had already visited and told the woman who ran the place that their horse was 'quirky' about going out in the field. They had then been told that they could have a post and rails paddock with one other horse who was very quiet so would not, at least, gallop with her. They had already installed her rubber mats into the stable allocated to her, after some help from James with a Stanley Knife to get them to fit; inevitably, the stable was smaller than the vast foaling box she had at Ainsty.

This one was within a barn of stables. She had horses stabled at either side of her and then could look out and see horses that were stabled in front of her, so she settled remarkably quickly. Ingrid took her into the indoor school that very day and Alira schooled well, becoming looser in her shoulders now and lighter on the hand, really appreciating the space which let her make use of the full scope of her stride; for a little horse she covered a lot of ground!

That night, Lucy and Ingrid were exhausted but excited, chatting about the prospects that this new home held for them.

"There are competitions here, and an outdoor as well as indoor schools. She will learn so much, she will be working alongside other horses more often which will build her confidence..." Ingrid stopped as Lucy made a face.

They had unhitched the trailer from their truck (ancient four by four purchased on account of the need to be out on the roads in all weathers) in order to go for a last load – their hay – and now could not get it hitched on again.

"We need to move it. We have to keep trailers round the back there. Oh no, this might take a while," Lucy whined.

They had been on the go for many hours and darkness was gathering.

Ingrid said, "It's a good thing we started out early this morning!"

This had been essential given that Alira had decided to stand on the ramp of the trailer for an hour and a half, refusing to load, while Lucy coaxed, stroked and finally pleaded with her to get in the trailer!

They knew from practicing many times that starting a fight was fruitless, the mare would just get more and more upset and there was simply no contest when it came to who was strongest. Patience was required and on this particular day it was imperative they got going and got sorted, but horses have this peculiar way of reacting to that urgency and Alira in particular would not entertain being hurried. They even tried walking Monty through the trailer to see if she would follow. But why would she? She did not even like him and he seemed quite nervous as well. Lucy just kept on trying, refusing to give up, patting, pushing, even singing to her! She did win in the end!

That day seemed to go on forever and Lucy's need for sleep became all consuming. They managed to get to bed eventually, only to be down at Normanton early the next morning to see if Alira was okay. She was slightly 'tucked up', looked skinny, but was bright and alert although not too wired. The Equestrian Centre where they now were stabled was owned by a blustering young woman and her much older aunt, the latter immediately took an immense liking to Alira.

When Ingrid went to ride, the older lady offered to teach her, for she was a dressage judge and instructor. After an hour of work, horse and rider were both sweating but happy, they had worked across trotting poles to try and lift the mare up from her forehand; a good understanding was being developed between teacher and pupil. Cooling Alira down, Lucy led her about the sprawling premises to familiarise her with her new surroundings. The instructor was leaving the indoor school and upon seeing this she laughed, "She fell on her feet when she found you two, didn't she!"

She was already aware that this was a beloved horse who had her every need attended to. This did not mean that swords would not be crossed with the instructor, Tamara, but the friendship between her and the two women was to ultimately stand the test of time. Alira's magic had worked on somebody else and the horse could not frighten this determined and knowledgeable woman.

The weather turned again, from promising spring to cold, damp, dull days with snow and sleet, but there was a milder edge to the weather down here as compared to up in the hills at Ainsty, which Alira enjoyed – perhaps it felt more akin to her original home, so much further away to the South. The environment suited her and on the worst days they had the joy of working indoors, also Ingrid had found a flat locally, so Alira was not left for such long days before seeing her owners, although Lucy arrived later because she had to drive a greater distance than before, at the end of her working day.

Ingrid would have got busy and sorted her horse out ready to ride, Lucy would work with her in one of the schools if they were on their own, or just watch if others were riding too. Many of the other liveries were young women about Ingrid's age. Ingrid was to make some good friends; there was a man who was working at the higher levels of dressage with his huge chestnut gelding, Kentucky. The schools were also available to hire, so many horses and ponies were always in the yard or the schools, being ridden and jumped, loading and unloading from horseboxes and trailers. Alira was getting a fine education in the ways of the equestrian world. She settled well into this new style of life and her owners were always proud of her, for she received many positive comments about her looks and her movement.

Alira was still a problem in the field. The Equestrian Centre offered to have one of their staff turn out horses so that owners could come and give horses hay, short keep (their 'breakfast'!), get the stables mucked out and then go to work, knowing that horses had eaten before going out into the fields and so would be calmer during the day, before being brought in before evening stables. The girl who was initially given the job of putting Alira out was tall and strong, but rotund, shaped actually quite like a ten-pin bowling skittle and Alira thought the game was to knock this unfortunate skittle over. The poor girl would battle her down the alleyway between the electric fenced fields and upon getting to the gateway of her area, Alira would whip round and knock her for six.

Away the mare would go with the rope trailing from her head collar, and then time would be spent catching her to take that off, hopefully before she stood on it and gave her neck a nasty jerk. Obviously, this could not continue, it was a wet spring and the girl kept coming back to the yard covered in mud. Tamara had little sympathy and gave her advice, but none of it helped. Ultimately, Tamara herself took Alira down to the field and fought Alira's impulse to gallop away with every fibre of her wiry body, amazingly never losing hold of the mare. Alira of course increased her rebellion and would stand up and rear, but fearless Tamara would go right in, between her front legs and elbow her in the chest, remonstrating, "Get down!" And finally would free her in the gateway of her piece of field. The owners of the centre took great care of their land, because they hosted cross-country events and needed British Eventing to approve the state of the course. Alira's hooves were making unwelcome divots once more.

Anita had suggested pairing Alira with Jonjo a quiet old gelding who, she said, would never gallop. Ten days later, people were walking over to see the field, having witnessed that oh yes, Jonjo could gallop and did, with Alira! The field was a narrow strip of a big pasture and where all the other strips were green. This was just a sea of brown mud, from the two horses tearing up and down, Alira in the lead and Jonjo manfully trying to keep up. Sometimes, witnesses reported, she galloped all day. Lucy and Ingrid were anguished that she might strain tendons in her legs, but she remained sound. The problems she was storing up for the future were hidden from them now, but they kept trying to find some field arrangement that would make Alira be calm.

They were lucky that Tamara had a soft spot for Alira. Tamara herself had an old mare who had once had Alira's alacrity and presence and the woman would have loved to have Alira all to herself. Hence, she was prepared to offer that Lucy and Ingrid's mare could share a fenced paddock near the yard, with the older mare. This was a dry area with little grass and consequently was used as a car park when shows took place, so it would only be a temporary arrangement, but immediately improved her behaviour when turned out there. She seemed to like the older mare, who kept her in her place with timely bites and kicks when Alira tried to set off, but no real damage was done.

When a competition happened and the field was used as a car park, Alira had to stay in, fretting in her stable all day, her poos would become loose and her coat would lose its shine. Ingrid worried about getting on her back after time indoors, for Alira would be sharp, have her back up and tail swishing. Lucy was less worried about her but did realise it was hard for the mare that the other horses were turned out and she was left in by herself. They were offered another companion, an old gelding who actually was lame and could not gallop, but he became overly amorous when she was in season, so they had to be parted!

Alex was becoming a good friend to Ingrid. They had a love of horses and dressage in common and he was a polite and sociable man. He offered to let them turn Alira out with his big horse, Kentucky. Alex was friends with Anita and Tamara, who ran the centre, so had the privilege of having what was known as the 'Show Field' for his horse. Once again, the field would not be available when there was a show, but often horses could stay out behind an electric fence to one side of the Show Field. This was to mean a fantastic education for Alira, watching ponies and horses scurrying about, jumping and so on; but first they had to establish calmness – nobody wanted hoofmarks all over the show field!

Alex was a body builder as well as a dressage rider, a roofer who kept a constant tan and was quite a magnet to the female sex. This made Lucy determined to be carefully polite, although friendly and not show any signs of responding to his charm. Ingrid was more susceptible and Lucy did not see what was happening right under her nose. Lucy had seen him holding Kentucky when the horse threw a tantrum inside his trailer; basically, the man planted himself, demonstrating mighty biceps as with one hand he held the huge animal – Kentucky was cantering on the spot but was unable to escape.

Alira was always turned out by Ingrid herself now as this was the best way to ensure that the horse had a predictable routine, which seemed essential to keep her sane. It meant Ingrid had to be up very early every single day. When Alex saw the behaviour of the mare going into the field, he was concerned for Ingrid's safety for Alira still whipped away with a mighty bound as her head collar was released.

The following day, Ingrid took Kentucky, the bigger but calmer horse and Alex led Alira out to the field. This was one horsey man who actually taught Alira something which she remembered for the duration of her time at Normanton; when she tried to go he held her. Not only that, he made her back up and wait until he was prepared to let her go. Over the next few days, he had some physical fights with her, until she was prepared to wait patiently for her release. This contributed to reducing the galloping behaviour in the field too, she was calm at the outset and then Kentucky's large, calm presence made her feel safe; he was the dominant one in the field.

Still, there were complications when Alex wanted to take Kentucky away, to ride him or for competitions. Then Alira was no longer calm and went back to careering up and down, flying over a small hill that was in the otherwise flat Show Field, leaping off it from half way down, turning at lightning speed when she encountered a boundary fence or hedge. There was no tolerating this now and Ingrid was in despair until she found an answer. A companion pony for their crazy horse!

The first of these was Boy Scout, the most charming little Shetland pony, with the typical short legs, general hairiness and huge forelock, through which it looked as if he would not be able to see. Boy Scout was on loan from a friend whose little sister had outgrown him; the mare arched her neck when she saw him, blew down her nose onto him and Boy Scout remained indifferent, no squealing, just a calm acceptance that this may be a new big friend. Nervously they turned them out together the following morning; Boy Scout was largely motivated by food so began to graze quite promptly. Alira looked at him in amazement then followed suit. Breathing sighs of relief, they left for work, asking anxiously how they had been when they returned that night, to be assured that there had been no galloping. The plan was working!

Only until the grass was being eaten away. The trio, who one particular day made escape, were Alira, Boy Scout and

Kentucky. Imagine Ingrid's horror when she arrived after work to find no horses in the Show Field! Then distant silhouettes were discerned by her as three creatures raced across the skyline, part of the cross-country course; a tiny one in front, a great big one behind, followed by a graceful one cantering in pursuit.

"Oh hell!" shouted Ingrid, only to clamp her hand over her mouth as she realised that Anita would be furious to have three renegades on her precious cross-country course.

Lucy dashed to the gate to retrieve head collars and was away in hot pursuit, grabbing a couple of friends to help her. They managed to coral the escapees by a water jump and led them back to the yard undiscovered. But how had they got out? Ingrid, Lucy and Alex always checked the fences religiously and now Ingrid and Alex tramped around the field to no avail, all seemed firmly in place with no holes.

Perhaps it was a good excuse or perhaps it was good horse management – that you stand in the dawn and just watch your horses' behaviour – Alex and Ingrid were getting closer and before they left for their working day, not many people had arrived at the livery yard. There was the opportunity to secretly give each other quite a lot of attention; neither of them wanted to start tongues wagging, but they were two attractive, extremely personable individuals who were instinctively drawn to each other. Add to that the simple animal feeling of desire when two such fit and healthy people spend a great deal of time together, by necessity in their case, both having high maintenance horses that required many hours to be spent with them. Both of them had just come out of difficult relationships, so were cautious, but lonely.

Anyhow, this next morning after the escape of the three musketeers, they were watching them after they had been turned out. Boy Scout quickly assessed that there was not as much grass in their field as the one next door and traced the ground with his nose, along the wooden fence perimeter, saw his opportunity, which was a gap far smaller than he got down and rolled under the fence!

Now they knew how he had got out and now he was causing Alira anxiety, she was galloping alongside the fence wanting to join her little friend. Kentucky did not want Alira to leave and he was quite prepared to jump out, he was an ex-showjumper, after all. Ingrid did not know whether Alira could jump, but Lucy had told her that once, going to get her out of the car-park field. Alira had cantered diagonally across the field towards her, making neat work of a crossed pole show-jumping fence that stood in her way!

Ingrid and Alex retrieved Boy Scout from the next field in order to prevent any more breaking out from the show field, it was clear that he would have to go back to his owners. Another friend would have to be found for Alira, when she was without Kentucky. Alex mentioned that he was house sitting for Tamara, he would be on site for the next couple of weeks and knew of another Shetland pony they could go and see. Two weeks is not long but was enough time for romance to blossom between Alex and Ingrid. The house gave them a place to meet where they thought nobody would see them. Ingrid and Alex were sometimes distracted from improving their dressage work to increasing their knowledge of each other. The horse world is notorious for gossip and they were naïve to think that no one would notice their liaisons; soon, it was the talk of the yard and beyond, that the two dressage riders were doing more than dressage together!

The other Shetland turned out to be unsuitable because it was too wild, so Ingrid had the idea of approaching a charity to re-home a pony as a companion. This proved to not be as easy as it might appear. People from the charity had to come and assess the livery stable, Lucy and Ingrid's intentions and knowledge, then there was a wait for a suitable pony, which was the charity's choice, not theirs.

Finally, 'Kerry' arrived, in a huge eight-horse horsebox belonging to the charity, all alone and invisible behind the stalls of the juggernaut. The little mare was very thin but looked reasonably well, although Lucy immediately noticed that hair was missing from the insides of her hind legs; when she queried this, she was told it was just because she was changing her coat. They kept her in for a couple of days, before putting her out with Alira; they had no worries for the pony's safety as Alira was so sweet tempered with other horses but wondered how the pony would behave and whether Kentucky would accept another mare into 'his' field. Kentucky was more than happy and started to parade around like a stallion, a harbinger of doom overlooked at the time, if anything it just caused amusement. After some sniffing and squealing, the two mares settled down together to graze side by side. Kerry was bigger than Boy Scout had been and there was no chance she could get out of the field.

Kerry was with them for a while and served her purpose, but then began to get more and more ill. They had to get the vet and it turned out she had some major kidney problem, so she eventually went back to the charity to end her days with them providing care. They could not keep turning her out to grass because her acidic urine scalded the grass and that was what had scalded her legs, hence the absent hair. Once again, Lucy and Ingrid were having to juggle fields and partners for Alira when Alex and Kentucky were away competing, which was happening quite often now as they were at the top of their game. Kentucky had gone up through the levels with his dressage, working from Preliminary competitions through Novice, Elementary, Medium to Advanced Medium and Advanced that led to Prix Saint George.

Alex was rather proud of himself when he could wear a top hat and long jacket, self-consciously making sure Ingrid saw him in his kit. The fact that some woman had gone to some dressage competitions with him had not escaped her, nor had Lucy been unaware of it. She did know now that there was something between Alex and Ingrid and at this point warned Ingrid to be careful. He was quite a lot older than she was and Lucy was beginning to know a bit more about him – for instance, that he got free livery by doing some jobs for Anita, that he did jobs for all sorts of people and worked on a cash-only basis. She wondered was he a free loader who would cause her daughter to get hurt? But Lucy knew she was powerless to intervene really, they were two adults who would decide their own fate!

When Kentucky was away, Alira would have to go back into the car park field sometimes. Tamara's old mare was a good influence on her, but a young mare was introduced, which had been bought for Tamara's niece. She hounded Alira and that relationship had to come to an end when Lucy went for her mare to find her trapped in the corner by this new horse, who was repeatedly kicking her with both hind legs, while Alira never kicked back! She only defended herself with the use of speed, in that way she could outwit other horses, but she was a pacifist like

108

Lucy! Alira was not prepared to get physical to prevent bites and bruises, the most she did was pull a shoe off while galloping at speed to avoid another horse. She kept losing over-reach boots too. Lucy and Ingrid were more than ever determined to find her a suitable companion.

Whilst all this was going on, Alira's ridden work was getting better and better, Ingrid was riding her every other night and having initially being embarrassed by her and her mount's lack of finesse, was now delighting in the admiration which Alira attracted, for her beauty, her movement and her sheer charisma. There had been difficulties and challenges about getting the mare's feeding right, too much food and she was too hot-headed and strong, too little and she suffered from 'tying up', which is where a horse has a kind of mild colic and can experience distress from an acidic gut. Haylage was like rocket fuel for her and made her stools very loose, so that had to be abandoned, lots of things that horses love had to be strictly rationed, like apples and carrots.

However, at last, they found a balance of some chaff with a few concentrates plus ad lib hay, then their horse looked like a show winner, her coat gleaming, her muscles beginning to give her the appearance of strength and solidity, while her agility was increased by the freedom in her joints and ligaments. She was still not always an angel though; her seasons had started with the spring and they made her restless in the stable and temperamental when ridden.

These times made Ingrid disillusioned with her. "She is heavy on my hands, leaning on the bit and setting her jaw!" She complained to Lucy.

"Talk to Tamara about it in your next Monday Club," replied Lucy, a little exasperated that so many positive aspects were still leading to complaints from her rider.

But then, Ingrid was ambitious and perfectionist and wanted nothing to mar their presentation as a well-schooled dressage horse and rider, ready to compete again and perhaps even be placed in the first few horses. The potential was so obviously there that it put pressure on Ingrid to fulfil that.

Lucy was just thrilled when she took Alira for walks, around the premises, down the lane, usually in hand but occasionally on her back! The summer weather helped Lucy's aches and pains and when one night she rode Alira down the lanes to the nearest village, she felt it did not get much better than this. The evening was so calm it was surreal, the hedges were green and the trees verdant with foliage.

Her horse was watchful, attentive to her aids, had that spring in her step that made her movement hypnotic, perhaps not good for Lucy's neck but she did not care about that right now. They trotted on the smoother bits of track and smartly up the road, they turned and came back and she felt on top of the world as she rode back into the yard, one of a fraternity of people who own horses and ride them, rather than one who is a groom, even if she is an owner!

Alira was always nervous on their excursions and when she had her in hand. Lucy had to be light on her feet, ready if she shied or got in a panic about some distant thing which she could not discern properly. These distant monsters often caused no further concern once Alira had worked out what they were. She was getting braver and bolder about all manner of things; Lucy had led her down the lane to the main road and let her graze while fast traffic went past, had passed fields with sheep in, dogs and bikes. Then a show took place for coloured horses, which Alira could be frightened of, maybe because they could be cattle? But Lucy led her all around, there was noise, flags, a generator and music and she was fine, no misbehaviour, just intelligent interest in what was taking place.

Such was her demeanour that when a Trailblazer's Show took place at the Equestrian Centre they entered some in-hand showing. The day was tremendously exciting and fun; she won first in the 'Horse in Best Condition' class then first with Ingrid running her up in hand in the best Sports Horse class, was Reserve Champion of the show. This was slightly unusual in that she had won her classes and yet a horse who was in second place to her became champion! Even so, her owners were leaping up and down, jubilant that they had produced their horse to a standard that was recognisably good. Also that she was seen to have conformation that was correct and suggested she had a future in equestrian spheres. The rumour was that the owner of the horse that received the Show Championship had complained because Alira Compliquer was not presented appropriately in that she had her whiskers still on! Lucy and Ingrid were aware that it is conventional to shave off extra hair for showing, unless of course you were showing a Mountain and Moorland breed, but felt that such a sensitive, nervous horse could not do without her whiskers, her 'sixth sense'.

Ingrid wanted to do dressage with her horse; but felt that she was not ready yet. Alira was heavy on the hand in canter and too strong for Ingrid to place her accurately to the letters required in tests. This demonstrated that the mare was too much on her forehand, not balanced enough to use her power from her hind legs and lift up in front.

Battling with her in the indoor arena one day, Ingrid met a lady riding a huge black mare called Lady Jet – an Oldenburg! They chatted excitedly and soon realised that Lady Jet was Alira's cousin! Her rider had paid to come and use the arena as she did not have a good surface to work on at home and was having trouble with her horse being strong in canter, almost the same problems that Ingrid was experiencing with Alira. Her cousin was older than she but had been as difficult to bring on as the other mare, resorting to a spectacular rear when she did not want to comply. The two women quickly exchanged phone numbers and Natasha, the other older woman, vowed to come back and, if necessary, help with Alira's training.

This was fortuitous as Natasha was a highly experienced dressage rider and could perhaps understand Ingrid's problems more than Tamara could, having trained one so similar to Alira in temperament.

Chapter 15
Summer of Indecision

Ingrid wanted to make sure her horse was not being strong for any physical reason, so arranged for a local dentist to come and check her teeth. The lady who came filed her back molars and made her mouth a bit sore, so Alira had a couple of days off but soon recovered. Not long after this, Ingrid went on holiday and Lucy hoped she would come back with renewed confidence – but no. She could not understand why Ingrid was so distracted, seemed low in confidence and full of self-doubt. When women are like this there is often a man involved and sure enough, Ingrid talked to her mum about it eventually; Alex had asked her to do evening stables the other night (get Kentucky in, feed him) because he was going out with Rosanna!

"But, but – I thought we are together?" Ingrid had cried, only to be met with some muffled excuse that he was too old for her.

Ingrid liked Kentucky a lot so had done evening stables for Alex, but with a heavy heart and hoping that this would be a one-night stand.

Foolish girl! thought Lucy, as her anger with Alex increased.

Then more so as Ingrid told of how Alex had said again how he thought he was too old for her, but could not stop his feelings for her, so was stringing her along. Rosanna had been and gone but then there were others and at last Ingrid told him that she wanted no more to do with him, which was making it very hard because their horses shared a field and sometimes it made sense for whoever got one to get in the other. Kentucky was big but even when alarmed was not as sharp as Alira. He would piaffe and passage beside the person at his head, but not defy the lead rope or the expectations of him.

Lucy felt her daughter's pain but knew there was not anything she could do. *The hardest part of being a parent,* she thought, *is not all that you have to do for your children, but when you cannot do anything and have to watch their pain.*

She was thankful and so was Ingrid, that they had a horse, which at the end of the working day, absorbed her completely while she rode and trained her. She could forget that she felt a fool and totally focus on the rhythmical stride of her horse, gradually getting her to be supple, obedient and to accept the contact of the bit without fighting or fussing.

The progress of training was halted when minor injuries necessitated one or two days' rest. Alira caught her hock on a caravan which Anita put in the field without telling either of them and inevitably the mare's curiosity led to investigation and then probably being startled and rushing away, catching her hock on the tow bar as she went.

Natasha started to come quite regularly and give lessons to Ingrid and Alira; leg yield, shoulder-in, turns on the forehand, medium trot was all excellent but the canter was still unbalanced.

While Ingrid was riding by herself in one of the indoor schools, Lucy could see that their mare looked like a fit racehorse, but during the session, she would stare about and be silly, lean on the bit and not listen to the aids, fly off in canter and be difficult to manoeuvre. Tamara refused to give any advice, having taken offence because Natasha was teaching her beloved little horse; but not just that, her beloved Ingrid. People around horses are emotional and unpredictable – a bit like the horses they ride!

Anyway, Natasha was very helpful and gave Ingrid tips about how to stop Alira being a tearaway and also encouraged her to start competing; Preliminary tests do not ask for advanced balance and carriage.

"Get the little horse out there and give it a go!" recommended Natasha.

Ingrid procrastinated; hesitating because she feared her horse would leave the arena, rear up, gallop away! Yes, Alira could do any of these but not as much now, she was not as recalcitrant, not as nervous, or petulant or defiant.

Ingrid sent off the entry form.

Part 2

Chapter 16
Finally! Off They Go

The haunting call of an owl before dawn made Lucy aware that she had to drag herself out of bed. She remembered it was a competition day! Her arms ached from carrying buckets of water down the yard to wash her mare's tail, grooming her shining brown body and polishing the saddle and bridle the night before.

Lucy and Ingrid were not inclined to wash down all the time in case it removed the natural oils in her coat; they believed that nothing was a substitute for regular, thorough grooming, but they had bathed her once during the summer. They had tied her near the tap and got warm soapy water and washed her head to toe and then a rinse – she had cast from side to side and pawed the ground but was not really concerned, quite enjoyed the rubbing of her mane and skin. She stood looking dark and dangerous, all her hair flat down, kicking her belly as drips coursed down her side, swishing her tail and drenching Lucy and Ingrid in doing so. She quivered the muscles over her withers and shook her head as the drips ran down her forelock. When the bath was finished Lucy had run up the yard with her and Alira got really excited about her wet cleanliness and seemed to want to play! She bucked and kicked, pawed the air and skipped, sure something exciting must be going to happen after all this fuss!

Today, something exciting actually was happening. Ingrid was competing her in a preliminary test. Lucy dressed and drove with the rising sun behind her towards Normanton. She had kissed James goodbye, but he was still asleep, a 'horse widow' again, he would joke. Having a horse was a test for their relationship. The commitment to hours of work spent caring for an animal, then time spent watching Ingrid riding and helping her develop her technique, meant that they got little time for each other but their partnership was one of decades and had actually begun with a long separation whilst James was in the army and stationed abroad. Lucy was expecting Sophie at that time and the birth was imminent when he returned! Their reunion was one of delight and over the years, trust and devotion had developed, but they each protected their freedom and valued independence always, even though they cherished time spent as a family.

The many challenges which parents face had been demanding at times but cemented their togetherness. The years of striving to make a living and keep a nice home for Sophie and Ingrid meant that they treasured time together but did not resent time pursuing their own interests. Lucy in particular loved time spent with horses and James rarely complained about something that made her so happy and enthusiastic.

Looking in her driving mirror, Lucy could see the rising sun behind her, all around, the land was awakening to what promised to be a bright day punctuated by spots of drizzle, when the sky would suddenly cloud over and hint at the grey days to come as autumn approached again. The mist of condensation on her windscreen suggested that it was cold outside; there had even been a thin crusting from an early frost on her car that morning.

Suddenly, a young hare darted across the road. She braked cautiously, but need not have, for it was gone into the opposite hedgerow in the blink of an eye. Lucy reflected that it was one of the lucky ones that had escaped the sharp blades of huge farm machinery that harvested the arable crops. All around, nature was busy with life, a hedgehog crossed the rough track that led to the Equestrian Centre, perhaps searching for a winter retreat.

But now the sun was out again and the smile from her daughter was even brighter when she entered the yard. Ingrid was full of enthusiasm but also anxious about the evaluation of others, not least the judges who would score her performance.

"She is fed and I just need to start plaiting her mane," she called to Lucy.

"Oh great, I will get on with grooming," she replied.

The yard was filling up with horseboxes of every size, some very smart with flashy horses inside, unloaded by people who looked confident and relaxed, neither of these emotions were being experienced by Ingrid, but she was trying hard not to convey any anxiety to her mare, who was already aware that something was afoot. Alira stood in her stable with ears pricked and her lips just twitching slightly; alert to the vibes around her.

The day went well for Team Alira. James came down near the time for Ingrid's test and watched a well-behaved little horse, looking extremely smart, doing her stuff as required. Ingrid remembered her test and did not need to have it read out to her, which added to the impression of fluency and unity between horse and rider.

Ingrid felt a surge of energy from the mare as she went into the arena, under the eyes of the judges and thought, *I must contain it, sit deep, stay calm, let her move.*

Move she did, for she certainly could, every stride to its maximum, showing her freedom of movement, but sometimes sacrificing accuracy as she strode past the letters. Maybe a jiggle in the walk, perhaps a bit too much restraint on the trot as Ingrid ensured that she did not break into canter and certainly a bit too much enthusiasm for the canter, the mare thundered around the arena! But Ingrid could bring her back to trot and then walk, but in the 'free walk on a long rein', she did not stretch her neck and relax as she should have but fussed with her bit and dropped behind the contact, meaning that the transition to trot again was abrupt and not quite controlled.

But at the end, she went smartly – and straight – up the centre line, to halt squarely in front of the judges and allow Ingrid to drop her head and right hand in salute. They came out of the arena very happy, Alira looking smug as if she thought she had won, Ingrid just pleased with the standard of the effort they both had put in. Ready to compete again.

The next competition was at a small but renowned riding school about twenty miles away, so this time they had to allow time for loading and a trailer journey. Alira was filled with horror when Ingrid produced travel boots; big sort of leg warmers to make sure the horse does not knock itself while travelling. Her action as she walked to the trailer was comical, lifting her legs as if stepping over an obstacle at every stride. There was some reluctance to go in and then apprehensive whinnying as soon as her owners left her to get into the truck. This continued as they advanced slowly down the drive, passing the field where some of her colleagues were grazing. They called back to her and she banged her feet about, was told to settle by Ingrid.

Then as Lucy increased her driving speed, the mare journeyed well until she resumed her noise at the advent of a slowing down and the sense that more horses were in proximity, as they approached the venue. She was unloaded quickly and walked in hand by Lucy while Ingrid raced off to register her arrival, confirm the time of her test and collect her number. Lucy talked to Alira as she led her around, reassuring her that she could be calm and was safe, gradually relaxing her and enabling her to establish where she was and what was happening.

Another quick rub down and brush of her tail, then Ingrid mounted and rode her into the warm-up arena, busy and full of various horses. She was to learn that there is an art to utilising the warm-up arena; to some extent not to draw attention to yourself because some riders, if they were threatened by the look and paces of the new Oldenburg horse that had joined them, would ride straight at Alira to unnerve her. So to some extent it was necessary to be bold and carve out a space to work, otherwise effective preparation was impossible.

They were learning; was it better to get in there and work the horse hard, like so many competitors did, or just keep her calm and loosen up a little bit? Ingrid opted for the latter, which seemed to work, for when she went into the arena, the extra adrenaline from leaving the other horses as well as perhaps sensing her rider's evaluation apprehension, gave Alira plenty of forwardness and impulsion.

The test began and Ingrid performed a straight, rhythmic trot up the centre line, then showed her horse's suppleness by a neat turn towards F, going well into the corner and bending Alira around her inside leg. Then she had a lovely contact on the bit as she embarked upon a twenty-metre circle. Ingrid could just see the corner of her mare's inside eye and used her legs to encourage that inside hind leg to step under. Next across the diagonal in a straight line, straightness was never in doubt, but surely, this Warmblood horse could show more activity in the trot?

Ingrid knew her mount and just could not ask for more or she would break into canter and lose a lot of marks for that movement; as it was she lost a few marks for lack of impulsion. Now she had to bring Alira back to walk, but Alira seemed to think, well, I have trotted, I want to canter now!

Consequently, the walk was not straight or in a pure four-time rhythm, the collection was not evident for the horse had grabbed the bit, although that is not too important at this level. Now for the trot up the long side and a canter circle to begin at C, hurray! Alira seemed to say and shaking her head put in some joyful bounds and was around the twenty metres required in a flash, too quickly for Ingrid to organise the next move, but she did, albeit late, her horse had gone past the letter. Finally, the turn up the centre line, square halt, except for the fact that she swung her hindquarters slightly left. Ingrid saluted the judge, receiving a broad smile from her; she could see Ingrid had her hands full with this charismatic horse!

Ingrid relaxed her hold on the reins and walked Alira around the edge of the warm-up arena, until she was cool and calm. Lucy finished off this task outside, then rubbed her down, having removed the saddle. They tried tying Alira to the side of the trailer, with a hay net, but she refused to settle unless one of them stood by her; the minute that they both left they would hear an anxious whinny and she would start casting about, trotting on the spot and half-rearing.

"I'll stay here," announced Lucy. "And you go to see if your results sheet is ready."

When Ingrid returned, she was smiling a wry smile, holding an A4 sheet of paper in her hand. They pored over the judge's comments.

"As usual," said Ingrid, "'Unbalanced in the canter', but some lovely comments about her paces, like 'pleasing trot steps', lovely little horse', then 'very well ridden'."

They put Alira back in the trailer, with some persuasion, she clattered in then started shouting 'Help' to her colleagues – high shrill whinnying, punctuated with a deeper 'Huh-huh-huh' to her owners upon hearing a voice from the truck window.

"All right, girl, you're okay."

Lucy had carefully and expertly reversed the trailer out of the yard full of horseboxes and trailers and they were on the road home.

Ingrid said, "I get so anxious in the warm-up arena but then I just love it when I'm riding the test and I can see her little ears in front of me. One pricked forwards, one flicked slightly back as if she's listening to me, she has got a nice, light contact on the bit and, you know, I only have to touch her sides for her to respond to my legs."

Lucy agreed and added that she was with her on Alira's back. It may be that she was watching from the gallery or wherever but it would always be that she rode every stride and gained joy vicariously from being a part of the preparation and then the competition.

They chatted on through the journey home, reflecting how they never did anything now, as in going out, swimming, reading books, other projects – their lives revolved around Alira. True, there were the two of them, so it meant that Lucy could cover for Ingrid when she wanted to meet friends, but most of the time, when not at work, one or both of them were at the stables.

Kevin, the farrier, claimed that Alira was the cleanest horse he'd ever shod, she was always presented so well, immaculately groomed, tack polished, never any of her bedding in her tail!

"I can't imagine what it was like to be without a horse now," said Lucy, "but I don't even miss having a lie in at the weekend or having time to shop, or anything. She just gives me the motivation to do everything, having a horse like her is magic."

Ingrid agreed, "At work, they don't know how I do it, get up so early, I mean, and do morning stables before I even start the drive to work, but it isn't that bad really, although I know it will be harder when the clocks change and its dark at both ends of the day again."

Lucy said nothing at this point. Sometimes when her back ached and her limbs felt like lead, she did not know how she did so much for that horse, but she knew she had a passion for the animal that was a fascination, an inspiration, almost an addiction; it kept her washing brushes, bandages and numnahs, cleaning tack, grooming, walking, lunging, yet she couldn't even ride. Alira now had a gentleness in the stable that was endearing and delightful, she was so affectionate and responsive.

Lucy knew that Ingrid had got a new boyfriend, not someone connected with horses but who clearly was not being put in any position of priority over Alira and would know the score from the start. The training and production of Alira was a priority in Ingrid's life!

They were nearing the yard now and Alira started calling to the other horses again. Ingrid announced that she did not mind that she had not won yet. "I just want to feel that she has improved and is getting better marks."

"Oh yeah," Lucy agreed. "It's just being a part of it all for me, definitely a dream come true just to <u>be</u> a person with a horse and have the excitement of going to a competition – and she always looks so good! Sometimes in the collecting ring I feel like most of the other horses are bigger than her, but then she starts working and you forget she's 15.2, she moves so well she looks 16.2!"

Alira was able to go out in the field when they returned. Kentucky was out, so they could put her with him whilst they put her bed ready in the stable, as well as feed and hay. Then they got her in and Lucy brushed off sweat, now with mud added to it for she had a good roll, then Ingrid rugged her up. Only then did they have time to grab something to eat and go home, fatigued but content.

This would go on forever and Alira would increase her scores every time – this was how they felt.

Chapter 17
Slow Progress

The autumn was drawing into winter and they were beset by many minor problems, even while the horse was proving to them just what great potential she had as a dressage horse with a beautiful, fluent style of movement. The arenas at Normanton – a full-sized indoor, a smaller indoor and an outdoor – all had great surfaces and enabled them to school her whatever the weather, but there were ongoing frustrations about the field arrangements and the stabling was not ideal.

During wet weather, the fields were unavailable and Alira was spooky, inattentive and difficult to ride when she had been in her stable all day. This was aggravated by her being anxious in the stable because the building was being re-roofed, with the horses inside! Most of them seemed unperturbed, but Alira was nervous and restless about what she could hear but not see.

One day, when the roofers were actually overhead, Anita put their mare in an empty stable with an uneven floor on which there was no bedding and Alira slipped, resulting in unsoundness for a couple of days.

Another day the hunt came past and upset all the horses, Alira in particular was partly excited and slightly terrified at the sounds of galloping horses, the horn and the baying of hounds. Lucy and Ingrid were against fox-hunting and were unable to see how tearing across the countryside could be justified in this day and age of intensive farming and rapidly declining flora and fauna, when it was supposedly against the law and created antagonism between equestrian people and the public. Ingrid learned how to get information about where and when hounds were meeting and then they had to use a mild sedative to keep Alira calm.

There was no opportunity to compete in December and the New Year began with bitter cold and hard frosts interspersed with periods of heavy rain. The horses rarely had access to the fields and feeding appropriately under constantly changing circumstances was challenging. For as soon as the weather improved, building work continued apace, imposing high levels of noise upon the stables area and as a higher roof was completed above the original roof, Alira's area became very dark, enclosed and damp, which had a detrimental effect upon her breathing. At one point, her head became swollen and her eyes runny. This had to be attended to by the vet, who prescribed anti-inflammatories. Complaints to Anita were to no avail, but the two women kept taking their horse out to graze on verges, walking her out and Ingrid gave her lots of riding; between them, they kept her reasonably well and happy.

March the third was a beautiful day, bright sunny periods interspersed by cloudy spells, but enough warmth in the air to suggest spring was on its way. This was the day that Alira was born, seven years ago. Appropriately for her birthday, she achieved the highest Preliminary class score so far in a dressage competition at Normanton; Ingrid was complimented about her rhythm, balance and behaviour. They were so proud of their lovely mare and it was all their own work that had brought her on to be such a star. They were competing in affiliated competitions now, which meant more rigorous judging, but actually Alira's marks improved; a combination of progress and judges with a greater appreciation of the scales of training and the mare's potential.

Ingrid aspired to do better and better and of course, she was the one who rode and schooled the lovely Oldenburg horse; Lucy had an incredible eye for a horse and was able to comment on the impression which the two of them made, but increasingly it seemed that Ingrid wanted more specific help to develop Alira's dressage further. Lucy saw an article in the paper about a local girl made good with a top-class dressage horse working at the highest levels and fortuitously it seemed that she was offering lessons. Thereby started a relationship that made a massive improvement to Alira and furthered Ingrid's riding skills; Miranda really understood Alira.

"She is such a baggage," she would say, when the mare was showing off her emotional, argumentative temperament upon being asked to do something new and difficult.

They were competing nearly every week now and Alira was near the top of big classes, they were taking her further away from home and she was dealing with challenging occasions where there were flags and flowers, bustle and noise. Lucy walked her first always, getting her to settle down and see the places which they went to, while Ingrid got numbers and checked times, sometimes got them a paper-cupful of tea, much appreciated after early starts and careful preparation.

Lucy was also on hand when Ingrid went for lessons, which were outdoors in Miranda's large arena, surfaced with light and springy rubber, encouraging extravagant action in her horses, but deep going for Lucy on the ground! Her legs would be aching, likewise her arms from holding the excited horse, but then she would go and sit in Miranda's little hut to watch the lesson – it always seemed to be windy but Ingrid was given a headset to wear so that Miranda did not have to shout.

Lucy would have Alira's quarter sheet on her knees to keep warm. She was busy learning too, as Alira developed more and more. She could do shoulder-in, shoulder-fore, travers and the opposite, renvers, where the horse moves in a straight line but with either haunches in or haunches out. Also medium trot, which belies its name in that it is an exaggerated, faster trot, a precursor to extended trot, where the horse would really throw her feet out, so that Ingrid could see her foreleg and the flash of a little white sock as the mare powered forwards. Canter and counter-canter, endless transitions up and down the paces, and turning, bending, circling, suppling her.

They got a small horsebox to make it easier to transport Alira about and had great fun loading themselves and their charge into it and setting off to travel to a lesson or a competition; the horsebox meant that their horse had superior travelling conditions, but she could still be choosy about loading into it. Soon after obtaining it, Alira was playing up on the ramp and stood on her own shoe which twisted upon her foot then as her weight came back down upon it two of the horseshoe nails pierced into the sole of her hoof.

A halt to the proceedings, again! The vet had to be called. He parred the foot, applied a poultice and gave her an antibiotic injection plus some painkiller. She had to be in her stable for five days, with a huge bed. Ingrid had to re-apply the poultice every day to make sure no poison had gone up into the hoof.

Finally, she was allowed out into the field with a layer of thick padding, then vet-wrap bandage over the whole hoof and duct tape over all of that to keep it all dry and in place. Boom! When she got through the gate she went for it, five days stabled and now she was bucking, kicking then into over-drive. But then she settled to graze with a little pony they had borrowed to keep her calm. The next couple of days followed this pattern, but on the third day of some field exercise, hail deluged down and she came in hopping lame, the dressing on her foot thick with mud. And so, after thorough cleaning, the repeated application of poultices had to begin again; this is known as 'gravel', where a tiny bit of dirt has got up into the hoof and has to be painstakingly drawn out with dressings upon the hoof with substances known to bring out any dirt and inflammation.

Another four days now where the poultice had to be changed every four hours– impossible with work commitments but they got as close to it as they could – the hoof had to be put in a tub of salt water and cleansed with hydrogen peroxide then dressed again. This was a performance, the most difficult part being to get her hoof into a bucket of water, many were sent flying before she learned to stand. She had to stay in another week after the hoof was dry and healing, then the farrier had to shoe her very carefully with the nails further apart than normal. Her first release was into the indoor school, whoopee! She did have fun.

The remaining days of that week, she did go out and did get ridden, with the hole in her foot packed; she galloped a lot in the field, even though they curtailed the size of the area with an electric fence. Ingrid's first ride after the mare's enforced vacation was disappointing, she found her crabby and reluctant to go forward into the bit.

This was overcome by Ingrid quietly riding her, deep and still, calmly insisting that she did have to work and move away from her leg aids, use her hind legs to work forwards into the hand. She was soon back into the outline which Miranda had told her to aim for, holding her onto the bit but quickly rattling her snaffle when she leaned on it.

Chapter 18
Prizes!

The beginning of May was unseasonably cold and appallingly wet. A fine, wetting drizzle persisted day after day, everywhere was muddy and it was too cold for the grass to grow as it should. Presenting the horse for competitions as beautifully as possible was a constant battle, to get the mud off her, dry her wet neck, keep the saddle from getting too wet and protect her long tail from the surface kicked up in the warm-up.

Alira did not like bad weather. It was cold too, but this particular day she was a saint, went into the arena with her little head down, one ear back as if listening to her rider. She strutted her stuff as if she was a dressage queen and Ingrid came out beaming.

Lucy was patting the horse's neck enthusiastically, "You must have a good score for that, she was a super girl! Well ridden too – here, I'll rub her down."

Before long, they had learned that they had qualified for the Trailblazers Championship, as well as getting second place. Lucy led Alira around to cool down sporting a blue rosette, the first of many which she won in her career.

Soon after that, the Equestrian Centre hosted its annual Spring Show; Alira was entered and had a long time to wait for her class. While she was waiting, the Triathlon took place, which involved shooting, scheduled to happen in the barn behind her stable. Lucy and Ingrid were not surprised when Alira took exception to this, whirling round her box and whinnying, making a mess and not placated by her owner's attempts to soothe her. Lucy led her out into the melee of people, dogs and horses, where she did seem happier but still on her toes, consequently attracting much admiration.

Yet again, another cold, wet day was upon them, so Alira got covered in mud when Lucy took her round behind the barn to find somewhere that was quieter. When Ingrid finally rode her into the arena they were not hopeful of her success, for this was a showing class, not dressage and not only did she have whiskers, she was not gleaming at all! Her coat was damp and she was streaked with sweat because of her anxiety, disgruntled by the weather and not impressed that she had to follow the other horses around, then quickly bored by simple walk, trot, canter.

Whilst standing in line for the judge to peruse, she showed what she was really made of by suddenly and inexplicably deciding to rear to her full height – not conducive to being assessed positively as the best 'Riding Horse'! Ingrid was relieved when they left the arena without further incident, for Alira had pulled her arms out as she tried to keep her steady behind the horse in front; her long stride meant she kept getting too close and having to be held back, not something she was tolerant of in the circumstances.

No more messing about in shows. They joined British Dressage and now competed only in affiliated Dressage competitions, certainly this mare's forte and the area in which she would be appreciated. The next competition gave them their highest scores so far and comments from the judge included 'A lovely horse', 'Pleasing trot tempo', 'Quietly ridden'.

Another lesson with Miranda which went extremely well raised their hopes and aspirations and made them feel thrilled with their beloved little horse who was so energetic and full of fire yet prepared to bend her will to Ingrid's commands and enable her rider to advance their capabilities and show herself as a beautiful, fluent mover with athleticism and power.

The month of June was no less wet than its predecessor that year, so her next competition was in deep and squelchy ground, although the sun shone upon them as they ventured into the first of two classes they had decided to do that day. The mare was excited but her behaviour was fabulous and she won first prize in a class of nine horses! Followed by first prize in a class of eighteen with a score in the mid-seventies, which was highly unusual at the time. Lucy and Ingrid hugged; their exhilaration was like electricity, lighting up the whole place, making everything that they did with their horse worthwhile, making everything seem like a dream. It was their serendipity.

After so much fog, mist and rain, it was fortuitous to find blue skies as they rendezvoused at the Normanton Equestrian Centre for the next two competitions which were being held at Hopeside, in a northerly direction up in the hills, but in a different area to that which Alira had become familiar with when she was at Ainsty. Hazy sunshine saw Lucy at the wheel, James and Ingrid both in the front of the horsebox, all setting out on the journey.

Initially, it was motorway driving which the horse found smooth and easy, but then they turned onto narrower, steep roads, all uphill, Lucy handling the driving with care as their charge had to adjust to the inclines.

"This is where it is good to know how to double de-clutch," she began, when Ingrid chimed in, "Oh, don't start that again, Mum, you tell me about that every time we go up a hill!"

They all laughed. "It's because she used to drive tractors," James justified her claims, but actually was glad of her driving skills as the roads got even steeper.

However, they arrived without mishap, very early because Alira would need to chill out and stretch her legs after the drive, as well as get used to her new surroundings.

"Look at that!!" shrieked Ingrid and they raised their eyes upwards to the hillside above where they had parked and there, towering above them was a huge windmill.

"Oh my god, whatever is Alira going to do when she sees that!"

Ingrid put the mare's bridle on then Lucy led her around the venue and to their relief and surprise, their horse seemed not to notice the windmill. Perhaps she would have if it had been turning, but the day was still and now hazy sunshine was gilding everything with gold. Rounding a corner to where she presumed the arena to be, Lucy was greeted with a shout as a woman appeared. "What are you doing?"

Lucy wanted to reply, 'what does it look like I am doing', but did not and replied sweetly, "Just walking our horse before the competition."

"Well, it hasn't started yet!" yapped the woman.

To which Lucy responded that she knew, but this was a young horse who needed to be calmed. The irritable woman seemed to accept that, but Lucy was amazed that somebody could be so ratty when actually she was receiving payment from them to enter! She was very glad of her intention to look around when she felt Alira stiffen and saw that there were cows and calves in a field adjacent to the warm-up arena.

The mare appeared to be less tolerant of these beasts so akin to her own species, than she was of windmills, so Lucy was glad of the bit in her mouth giving her a little more control than she would have had in a head collar. Going back to the place where the trailer was parked and Lucy and James were waiting, Lucy suggested that as soon as the arenas were opened up Ingrid should go and see if she could even get her in the warm-up, with those cattle situated in such close proximity.

Sure enough, when she got onto Alira, Ingrid could feel tension flowing through her horse's body; tension does not make for good dressage. Consequently, she worked at the end of the arena furthest away from the cattle. Her hands and legs and words all persuading the mare to go forward, to go calmly, to relax under instruction; not asking too much of her just yet, only expecting and hoping that she would forget the presence of cattle, that were monsters in her small horse-brain; just relax and listen.

Gradually, Ingrid felt her back go down and slowly felt her soften, started to ask her to bend and circle, do transitions – and soon, it was as if Alira had tuned into her aids, stopped fearing the cattle; one ear went back, she arched her neck to do her job properly. Next, Ingrid slowly expanded the area she was utilising; there were other horses there now and it was not long before Alira too, was working all across the arena, barely noticing the cattle and so was ready to go in to the school area where she did her test.

The sun was shining now and sweat shone on the mare's coat, Ingrid wished she could take her jacket off, but of course, British Dressage rules are that you keep it on, so she did not.

Two classes that day and she won them. High percentages again and the little horse was proud and smug when her owners let her know how delighted with her they were. Alira did not, however, think that going back into the horsebox was a good idea. She had been given a good long walk round by Lucy with her saddle off so that the sun dried the sweat on the mare's back. She had been brushed and offered hay, although she rarely ate in exciting circumstances and never when travelling.

Horses' faces are expressive and Alira's now clearly said, "Maybe not" when they asked her to go up the ramp.

Perhaps those hills had made it difficult for her, having to sit back towards the tail-bar, maybe she liked it at Hopeside, but whatever; she would go sideways, backwards, be stationary, but not go forwards up the ramp. James' strength was useful, he pushed her from behind, Ingrid pulled from in front, Lucy coaxed, cajoled and dug her fingers in where if ridden, she would get the message to go forwards, but no success.

"Looks like we are stuck here," then said, "James, what else can we do?"

Keeping calm was essential to keep the mare calm, so they decided to eat their sandwiches, for lunchtime had long gone, then try again. When they tried again, they succeeded because a kind person brought her horse into the box and out again. Alira followed this example, but was not allowed to come out again. James drove home and the two women discussed the preferability of a small horsebox over a trailer. The horsebox had been expensive, but it did mean that they did not need to run a diesel guzzling four by four and it made travelling a good deal more comfortable for nervous Alira.

They were now owners of a smart little blue horsebox, which was a van conversion so already had miles on the clock, making it more affordable. Crucially, the horse travels backwards in this type of vehicle and research has revealed that often horses prefer to be this way. Inside, their mare had a high breast bar, windows to look out of and a strong wall behind her to sit against going uphill or just to steady herself. Plenty of room and she learned then, while travelling, to splay her feet and sway with the movement, no longer as anxious or restless. This was if she finally decided to load into it, which at first was difficult. One of their first journeys in it was to Miranda's for a lesson, which went really well. But they had to add a couple of hours onto the time taken, just to get the damned horse into the box before going and when returning. Likewise, the next time, but then once again training had to be disrupted because a cough affected all the horses in the yard, meaning they could not go anywhere for fear of spreading it more widely. Their horse had to have antibiotics from the vet, as most of them did and riding was either abandoned or just a short bit of easy work to maintain interest.

When she had got over her cough, they went for another lesson with Miranda to get the mare working correctly again. After a good workout, where their teacher gave them no rest, Lucy walked the mare while Miranda and Ingrid chatted. The evening was sultry, dark clouds gathered overhead and the heat hung in the air like a threat.

"Better get her loaded before it pours down," Lucy suggested, heading off up to the yard where the box was parked.

Alira was having none of it. She was hot and angry about it, her ears were back in a fierce mare's face, as she plunged and threatened to rear. Miranda brought a lunge line which was passed behind her quarters and held a whip to threaten her – but she had never been whipped, so why would that make a difference?

"Oh, she is very silly!" said Miranda, very used to young horses, but finding this one particularly intractable.

"You wait there," said Miranda and took the mare by her bridle away to one side.

Her schooling whip was in her hand and she said, "You" and smacked her, "Are going to" and she whacked her again, "Behave," she laid two more sharp slaps along her side.

The look of horror on Alira's face was comical. She froze, looking absolutely astounded that someone could do this to her! Miranda marched her smartly and promptly back to the horsebox ramp, gave the rein to Ingrid and said, "Right! Straight up that ramp!"

Ingrid got her forward and front feet on the ramp, Lucy and Miranda drew the lunge line tight around her bottom.

"Go ON" growled Lucy – and with a clatter of hooves on metal she was up and in and being secured by Ingrid.

Everyone breathed a sigh of relief and they drove home in shocked silence, traumatised because someone had whipped their horse; but it had worked, she had gone straight in the horsebox! After that they always carried a lunge line and a whip with them, but amazingly, they never had any further problems with her. She started loading promptly and grew to like her horsebox, travelling happily further and further afield.

The colloquial idea of a flaming June did not materialise and the next lesson with Miranda involved a drive up the A1 in a cloudburst! The din of rain clattering on the roof of the horsebox and the swish of the tyres through surface water meant that Alira could barely hear Lucy's assurances through the little window behind the driver's cab, but she was fine, she was tall in her stall, alert to the sounds but was not reacting. Just occasionally, she would suddenly kick out behind, with a resounding bang on the wall behind the driver's seat that made Ingrid, who was driving, almost jump out of her skin! No 'fair weather rider' was she. She had her lesson in the pouring rain and horse and rider were soaked at the end of it. The instructor and Lucy could sit in the little hut constructed for the purpose, but Lucy was soon wet too, as she rubbed down her mare after the lesson, walked her, then rugged her up before the two of them loaded her without any trouble; she was glad to get in out of the rain!

The next competition dawned on a day that was actually dry, but the surface that Alira had to complete her test upon was heavy going. Alira achieved second place but was strong and difficult to ride. Then in the warm-up before the second class she had just relaxed, softened and opened her shoulders, when Lucy observed that she was not sound. Ingrid rode her across the school with a worried face.

"No, she does not feel right," she agreed.

They withdrew from the second class, took her home and turned her out in the field to enjoy the cool, but now sunny, day, with just enough breeze to ward off the flies that so persistently try to bite horses.

The next day, Ingrid trotted her up for Lucy and they acknowledged a slight lameness in the off fore, so that was followed by rest for a couple of days, then she was lunged because she seemed sound, schooled lightly the next day. The following day, while Lucy and Ingrid were at work and Alira was out in the field with Kentucky, some students of an Equestrian Studies course who were helping at the yard tried to move the two horses into another field, lost control of Alira and she galloped away down the cross-country course. She found her way back to the yard via the garden of Tamara's house and went to see the old mare, Bibby, then allowed herself to be caught and returned to her stable. Lucy and Ingrid were furious when they found a filled tendon on her near foreleg.

The frustrations of keeping her right and sound were made greater by a total lack of sympathy from Anita who ran the yard; she was very much a businesswoman and more concerned about maintaining her land for the yearly two days of British Eventing which she hosted. However, Alira was fine and well when they took her to compete at an influential Equestrian Centre which did focus mainly on dressage; as they left their place of stabling Alira had a tantrum, unsettled by her colleagues calling to her, but then she settled and travelled well, this time Westwards on good roads. Arriving at the venue, she heard other horses and started to bang rhythmically with her big well-shod hooves. Ingrid peeped through the window and saw that she was trotting on the spot inside her stall, very excited about another new place and clearly, a party going on! Lucy walked her about while Ingrid went to get her number and check times. Lucy was proud of her horse as she champed the bit and looked about herself, tense when she passed other big horseboxes and open gateways, which always spooked her.

"There's lots of competition today and the class is huge!" exclaimed Ingrid as she returned to the horsebox, neatly parked in a nice quiet corner.

That was a bonus, not having to park a trailer.

"You will be fine," said Lucy, noticing that Ingrid was pale under her make-up, her face in contrast to her black riding hat, her hair neatly coiled behind her.

"Just forget the judges and carry on with the schooling that you are going to do in the warm-up."

Ingrid felt better when she swung her leg across her horse and settled gently into the saddle, then joined the throng of horses working in the small indoor arena, dimly lit but with a light, firm surface, which Alira enjoyed. There was a challenge involved in just finding a space to work, then using the whole arena meant remembering to pass near side to near side. Also there were riders who cantered round as if they owned the area, making it unnerving to be near them in case of a crash. Then it was her turn to go and wait outside the main arena. Lucy took off Alira's boots and overreach boots, wiped away some foam from their horse's chest, a quick pat and they were in. A trot around outside the boards and then the bell rang; the test was to start.

Ingrid entered at a forward going working trot, straight up the centre line, feeling Alira's quarters lift behind her. Then curved her into a circle, aware of her horse's body bending through her spine and the elegant arch of her neck as she lightly held contact to the bit. As a result of which she was able to turn her at the side of the arena to trot across the diagonal, letting her horse stretch forwards and throw her feet out. Then circle again, unfortunately, not entirely accurately this time; but she carried on to bring her back to walk at the appropriate time, with a transition that lost none of her thoroughness and impulsion.

The medium walk was always difficult because Alira would so easily trot if urged onwards, but this time her walk was full of activity but showed regularity and purpose, without any jogging! Then to do a half circle and cross the arena again in free walk, which meant Ingrid must let Alira take the rein forwards and down and walk freely, for which she was never penalised for ground cover or freedom of movement, but did always hurry a little, eager to get on to whatever came next!

Another trot circle and Ingrid subtly prepared her mare for canter, enabling her to strike off on the correct leading leg exactly on the centre line and feeling the joyous bound into canter as she sought to regulate that big stride and keep her on the trajectory required. Before she quickly, it seemed, had to bring her back to trot again and allow her to stretch on the circle, which Alira did readily. Then she gathered her up to trot straight down the centre line again to a triumphant halt in front of the judges – and the mare stood square and proud, presenting the necessary square halt to allow her rider to salute the judges. A very good test and Alira's rider gave her a good pat as she walked out of the dressage boards then out of the arena as the next horse came in.

Now for a long wait to receive their scores, at a competition as busy as this, then an even longer wait to find out their position after the whole class had competed. Plenty to do though! When Ingrid came back from receiving her scores she was very happy and they got busy preparing Alira for the next class, wiping off flecks of foam for she always mouthed her bit, drying off any sweat, brushing her legs, wiping the tack. Ingrid had to change numbers while Lucy gave their horse a relaxing walk. Not much warm-up needed this time and Alira was in again, Ingrid this time being particularly careful to get the circles right and ensure that every movement was accurate and precise. Then Alira needed to cool down, hence be walked in hand. She was to untack, rub down, brush off, offer hay and water, put a sweat rug on and put back on the waggon. Ingrid returned from the Secretary's office, exultantly waving her score sheet and a blue rosette, second place even in that big class! Ingrid secretly knew that she had done better in the second of the two classes, but that did not mean that she would be placed, when there were many other good horses doing the test.

The mare was stood tall in her horsebox, the ramp was down so she could observe other people and horses. She was no longer sweating, but not relaxed enough to eat. She was anxious if both her owners left, letting them know by trampling and loud cries that started high and ended in deep notes from her broad chest; but as long as one of them was by her she would be content enough to stand, ears pricked, watching the proceedings. Lucy reached over the partition of the box, felt her horse's smooth brown muscular body and started to take out her plaits, which left her mane crinkled and curly.

Ingrid came back with exciting news. Alira's name was at the top of the leader board, but five horses were still to go, two of which were winning at Novice level, the next, more challenging level of class.

"Unlikely we'll beat them," was Lucy's measured response to her daughter, as she carefully removed something from Alira's eye; her heart felt full, to be here with a horse and her beloved Ingrid, now a woman and an accomplished horsewoman as well.

Time passed by and they had a brew from the café, in a paper cup, scalding and strong, but refreshing.

"Go and see if the rest of the scores are in," grinned Lucy, seeing that Ingrid was impatient to know the results.

She came back to the horsebox, her horse and her mother, with a beaming smile and this time, a red rosette! Alira had won the class, achieving first place, in front of more experienced horses and riders. They made a big fuss of Alira, until she started to get excited again! Then they put the ramp up and drove her back to her stable in some late sunshine. A merlin flew in front of them as they negotiated the rutted lane to Normanton Equestrian Centre, the bird appearing suddenly over the tall hedge, swooping down like an arrow then vanishing just as abruptly, with a smooth dive over the opposite hedge. Lucy felt happy. Happy to see the bird, happy to feel that they had arrived on the dressage scene, happy that Ingrid was so successful with this spirited mare.

Ingrid was full of excitement, buzzing from the day's events and doubly so because they had qualified for regional finals – so quickly! Her ambition grew and she visualised a red rosette, she and her mare flying around the arena because they had won at the regionals. There is no harm in dreaming, but dreams and reality are not always congruent.

July was mostly cool and damp that year; the trio of Lucy, Ingrid and Alira were to be found many miles away from their Northern home, competing at a championship which they had successfully qualified for by winning a particular class with Alira. This was a big adventure for them, for they took their mare away for three days and she had to be stabled overnight in pre-fabricated blocks amongst many other horses. She had withstood the journey really well, apart from kicking hell out of the box every half hour or so, then went into her new abode quite happily, astounding her owners; she got down to roll then calmly munched hay whilst observing the goings-on around her.

They agonised as they left her to go to their lodgings and were back long before the sun was up or the flies had started rising from the river to bite the horses. Lucy and Ingrid were both delighted to find her calm and happy, observing the other horses, then pleased to see them, which was confirmed by a deep whinny of greeting.

A couple of hours later, Lucy had finished grooming her mare and stood back to admire her. Alira was shining from tip to toe – from the delicate nostrils on her slightly mealy, soft nose, around her constantly twitching lips and her broad brown head with the little asterisk of white in the centre of her forehead.

Her mane was neatly combed onto the off side of her neck, which is not the conventional position, but it grew that way and would lie no other way! Lucy had made a neat parting between mane and forelock, just behind the usually alert pricked ears. They used to have fights with her about brushing her head, but no longer, she was amenable, would even drop her head and become bemused while her forelock was combed. There were so many things that had improved! She used to fight to be free when she was tied up, now she stood calmly, she would kick when her feet were picked up, now she would voluntarily lift them in anticipation, she used to barge across when being lead, now she walked alongside.

Her neck was sleek and shiny, well-muscled and beautifully curved; initially her neck had muscles in the wrong place, a result of occasional wind-sucking or crib-biting, when horses bite on wood and tense their neck, building up muscles underneath. The use of crib-stop and the fact that Alira felt safe and comfortable had stopped that habit, which she had appeared to learn from another horse when they were at Ainsty, when she was stabled for weeks due to all the snow. But now, her schooling had enhanced the naturally elegant curve of her neck and developed the muscles on top of the neck, making her look refined and accentuating the loveliness of her head. Somehow, she had the wide cheekbones and dished face of her Arabian ancestors, which had been used to improve the Oldenburg breed. Summertime gave her a lighter brown coat and the neat barrel of her belly was attractively dappled, but the dark brown remained across her rounded rump, powerful quarters, deep chest and down her legs.

Lucy had made her black tail gleam in the sun; it was long and quickly tangled again as often swished! Her forelegs were muscular at the top, flat knees, well-defined tendons, strong fetlocks, sloping pasterns; the off-fore was 'Lucy's leg', the only one that was black right to the hoof, which was also a black hoof. Black hooves are thought to be the strongest and that was the way for her. This moment in time captured her with her thin white socks bright white and the whole picture of this mare was one of perfection, strength and sweetness.

Lucy thought, *She will always be our horse, she will go from strength to strength and we will keep her forever, she will not look old until I am old.*

A quick pat and Lucy got on with getting kit out of the horsebox. Ingrid came back from emptying the barrow and started to put the short mane into plaits. This was an environment different to any show so far; hundreds of horses and ponies, all well turned out, all excited by the atmosphere, but mostly calm and well behaved. Lucy and Ingrid could hardly believe how well Alira was behaving and were unsure if it was just the reassuring influence of all those other horses or she was just so overwhelmed that she thought she had better do as she was asked!

When Ingrid got on her, Lucy walked beside them as they followed the tarmac footpath down to the warm-up arena. That took their breath away! The area was a maze of horses trotting, cantering, stopping, twisting, turning – how were they going to manage in here? Alira's eyes were wide and her head high. Ingrid gently applied pressure with her legs and in they went. To begin by walking the edge, then trotted daintily into the melee and began some transitions, suppling exercises and gentle yielding; nothing to wind her up, but just getting her attention and soon she was listening to her rider and was no longer phased by big horses cantering past and crossing her path.

Soon, she was called over to wait where the competitors entered the arena and the pair were able to see the huge space in front of them; six arenas, each with a single horse performing their test, the audience was small but was all around the periphery, the judges were in their cars, one at the top of each arena. Ingrid's stomach turned over but she quickly directed all her attention to giving the little horse confidence and making her aids clear, sitting deep and calm so that Alira was not overcome with the occasion and succumb to what would be a natural urge, to bolt out of the arena.

No such thing happened and the test was executed without mishap, then they had to do another test the following day, which resulted in enough points to be in the final placings, 10th, in fact, out of almost 300 horses. That day, the sun shone and ten horses and their riders went into the paddock to receive their huge rosettes, standing proudly to have the ribbons pinned to their bridles, then cantered round to the sound of Tina Turner singing *You're simply the best, better than all the rest.*

Alira thought she had won the whole championship and was so proud, arched her neck and threw her hooves before her, making Ingrid feel as if she was on a Grand Prix stallion and causing such pride in her mum, who stood applauding, that there was no stopping a tear from rolling down her cheek. They were on their way!

They were all so happy, (even the mare!) as they loaded up for the journey home. Lucy and Ingrid could not stop talking about every minute of every day as they drove away, so much so that they found themselves driving into the centre of Coventry, instead of the road they should have taken. Lucy pulled up the horsebox at traffic lights, in the middle of six lanes of traffic while Ingrid frantically tried to find the right directions on her phone. They thought that heir mare must be very scared in all this noise, with heavy traffic all around – but no, she was sound asleep in the back, her neck resting on the front barrier of her stall, her eyes closed – and that was the way she stayed, all the way back to the North of England! She had experienced so much excitement and seen so many things that she had never seen before!

They got her safely home and she tucked into her feed and hay; Lucy and Ingrid had to get back to the normality of work and life with a horse, constant needs, constant work, but constant joy and now always the plans for the next competition. Which was just two weeks later.

The day dawned bright and sunny but then clouded over with ominous rumbles of thunder in the far distance. Warm and muggy weather suited Alira, although thunder could make her a bit wired, but now it seemed she had decided to be a dressage horse and her behaviour was exemplary. The air smelt of musk mallow, lobelia and hydrangea which were blooming in Tamara's garden, a pair of buzzards circled lazily, then disappeared behind the grey clouds gathering in the distance. Alira went into the warm-up area, which was under cover and slightly dark; her coat gleamed enough to outshine the gloom and her modest warm-up showed her moving perfectly, white bandages accentuating the extravagance of her movement.

Into the arena and Ingrid had no nerves this time, just looked between those pricked ears and went into the arena with a purposeful trot up the centre line, knew when Alira arched her neck and dropped one ear back towards her that her mare was listening to the thoughts in her head and would respond to everything asked of her. When the first canter transition came, Ingrid's aids were light enough to be imperceptible, she literally just *thought* 'canter' and sat down, off they went into a perfect twenty-metre circle.

She won that class and the next one and by the end of the day, she had again qualified for the Regional Finals! Two weeks later, they took Alira on a journey to an important venue at an Agricultural and Equestrian college, where she won the Preliminary class and achieved second place in a big class which was her first Novice level competition. This venue caused Alira a lot of stress, because cattle and pigs were in the vicinity. The noise of them and the smell put Alira into a highly nervous state, but they had arrived in good time so Lucy walked their mare around, walked her and walked her. At first hard to hold, full of nervous fire and power, but gradually relaxing into the rhythm of her long swinging walk and attending to the reassuring voice of the woman beside her. When she went into the warm-up she was difficult for Ingrid to ride, but as soon as she went into the big indoor arena Alira forgot about everything outside and took on the demeanour of 'Ah yes, this is my job' and did a lovely test. She was not at all worried by baskets of flowers or flags and never spooked once, which many of the other entrants did and in the prize giving she stood proudly and obediently, with the attitude that it was all for her.

The stress of her day had affected her though, because the following day, when she was turned out, she was unsettled most of the day, galloping with Lincoln by her side, rain was falling and the wet mixed with her sweat making her coat dark and wavy. Lucy got her in and then gave her lots of walking, even taking her down the road, where she had to walk away from colleagues in the fields and even encounter sheep. Before the next competition came around she was settled again and this time Alira and Ingrid did two Novice classes, winning the first and qualifying for the Pet Plan championships as well as gaining fifth place in the other one, ahead of another thirty horses.

Alira and Ingrid continued their education into dressage, enjoying another lesson with Miranda, where they learned to do counter-canter. Going across the school in canter to turn and continue onto the other rein leading on the outside leg. Contradicting all of the earlier training where the emphasis was on ensuring that canter circles must have the horse leading on the inside leg. Horse and rider were dripping with sweat at the end of the lesson but triumphant that they had mastered yet another aspect of dressage, demonstrating that they could achieve balance, fluency and control.

The next test was in a long arena, which could have disturbed their equilibrium, but the mare seemed to relish the extra space to accommodate her long stride. They scored eight marks for counter-canter and secured second place with over 70%, even though they gained no marks for one movement where there was inaccuracy. There followed a period of rest because their mare had a cold. But as autumn changed the leaves to orange and red and brown they were off again, travelling in the horsebox and winning at the agricultural college, then again at a venue further away. By now, Alira was travelling well, although she got very excited beforehand and no matter how hard Lucy and Ingrid tried not to let her know that they were going anywhere she always sensed it somehow, even before her travel boots were brought out. She was going out each day with Kentucky and only occasionally galloping, she was flourishing in all her work under saddle and now could work with shoulders and quarters in or out, was starting half pass and her canter was becoming more 'uphill', flowed more easily from a prompt transition that appeared effortless.

Miranda's schooling arena was very deep – springy, but deep. Alira enjoyed her work in there, but later on, they wondered, had it asked too much of those low hocks and elastic fetlocks to work so hard in there?

Chapter 19
Outrageous Fortune

Many equine dentists are men, but when Ingrid heard of a woman who did the job and lived local to Normanton, she jumped at the chance to book a visit to Alira. The mare had been less enthusiastic about her hay, was leaving stalky bits and it turned out that indeed, she had a sharp molar, right at the back, difficult to access. On that particular day, Lucy could not be there, so Pam and Ingrid had to manage by themselves – a difficult task with that strong little horse, who objected a good deal. Afterwards, Lucy wondered if it was partly because she wasn't there; she had always been there, every time anything had to be done to Alira. Their horse had experienced dental checks before without being as feisty as she was that day; but anyway, the job got done and all appeared to be well.

Ingrid and Alira went on winning; a second and a first, a second and a third, a win with a massive percentage, by the end of that year they had done thirty-six competitions and been placed twenty-five times, earning eleven first rosettes, eight seconds and two thirds. For a young horse and an amateur rider with barely any previous experience, it was an amazing achievement.

The New Year dawned with leaden skies, damp conditions, snow and ice. Ingrid was not deterred and carried on having lessons with Miranda, learning the beginnings of pirouette, practicing shoulder-in, travers and renvers, counter-canter, many transitions between all paces. The horse and rider worked well but Alira was a real handful, she was fit now, did not like the cold even though she had a warm blanket over her quarters. Lucy was nearly always there watching, walking with their horse to warm up and cool down, but increasingly she felt that this was Ingrid's horse, their partnership was special, she was on the

145

periphery. But something was happening to the partnership, something was wrong.

Back at Normanton on yet another cold Saturday morning, Lucy watched their horse give a lacklustre performance in the schooling arena, her head nodding and shaking, the contact with the bit had been lost, was intermittent, she was unsettled, what had happened? The vet was called out, a week of rest ensued, antibiotics and painkiller administered for what appeared to be an ulcer in her mouth. She went out in the snow with Kentucky, played and fell flat! When Ingrid rode her again, she was brilliant, but still shy of her mouth and so there followed time in a bridle with no bit. This was not ideal for Alira and she was very strong in it and prone to her old habit of falling onto her forehand. Back into work properly again by February. But it started again, teeth gnashing and knocking, a constantly nodding head, ruining the appearance of fluency and consistency of her outline.

Unfortunately, the problem was not resolved when it was time for the regional finals, which everyone who had worked with the horse felt she could have won, but this just took the edge away from their performance. Alira behaved like a star in every other way, gaining third in the Preliminary Regional Final in a class of twenty-two and sixth in the Novice Regional Final in an equally big class. When it came to the prize-giving the first six horses were involved in the presentation and she stood there tall, proud and square, neck arched, sure that she was the winner whilst the other horses messed about and misbehaved. Then in the canter round she did it beautifully while other horses shied and bucked and generally made her look like the one who deserved to have won. Ingrid was so proud of her, but disappointed that this teeth knocking was limiting her chances. She was frustrated with repeatedly trying different bits, giving her special food, having her back checked, her teeth re-done... and nothing, nothing seemed to work.

Finally, as the rain poured down in February, they took her to have a CAT scan and found that she had a broken bone in her tongue. The veterinary expert questioned them closely and Ingrid remembered; when Pam had been treating Alira's teeth, the horse had reared up whilst Pam was holding her tongue – the woman did not let go. She had broken Alira's tongue and ruined the lovely contact that Alira had with the bit, which Ingrid had worked so hard to achieve, that had probably taken the regional championship from them and caused their poor mare a lot of pain. They sat in the waiting room of the veterinary hospital feeling devastated, glad that at last they knew what had gone wrong but horrified that they should be so unlucky; the vet said such an occurrence was very rare. The staff at the vet hospital had been extremely complimentary about Alira, saying she was the shiniest horse they had ever seen and recognising her beauty, but Lucy and Ingrid just wanted to know what could be done.

The vet prescribed a low dose painkiller because she did not seem to have too much discomfort except from the presence of the bit in her mouth. She was to have no bit in her mouth for six weeks, no treats by hand, no salt lick, no hay nets with small holes. Disconsolately, they loaded Alira back in the horsebox, impressed with the premises of the vet hospital, but not impressed at the long road to recovery that had been described. This six weeks was just to see if the bone might heal by itself, after which there were surgery options, as a last resort. Thankfully, these bills were covered by insurance, once Lucy had spent time trying to explain what had happened to their horse. The insurers were incredulous, never having even heard of a ceratohyoid bone, but could not argue with the scan pictures and the veterinary report.

The ensuing weeks were difficult, a bit of riding in a hackamore, lunging, going out in the field, walking in hand. Her hind legs filled as a result of being fit and not having enough work, so her feed was cut down and boredom became an issue for her, but they did their best and followed the vet's instructions exactly. They went back with her six weeks later and the vet felt there was improvement in that the inflammation in her mouth and throat had reduced, so prescribed a few more weeks, then suggested that they try riding her with the bit in her mouth.

Hence, it was well into spring when Ingrid got on her again, the weather was mild, lambs bleated in the fields and a distant curlew called its plaintive cry. Ingrid and Lucy had high hopes; she was a young fit horse, surely, the bone would have healed? Twenty minutes later, gloom had descended upon them, for the mare's mouth was open; she was knocking her teeth constantly and beginning to show signs of distress.

The weather was again beautiful on the day that they drew up at the veterinary hospital again, with Alira in the horsebox, to have the broken ceratohyoid bone removed. She came down the ramp looking for a party, but no dressage arena greeted her, just the neat gravel and concreted yard of the equine hospital. Swallows swooped, busy building their nests, a wagtail crossed in front of them with its awkward gait. Lucy and Ingrid agonised over the fact that here was this wonderful, perfectly healthy horse who was going to be operated upon for one tiny part of her to be corrected. There really was no other way forward though, a horse like her who could not wear a bit and was at the start of what they hoped would be an ascending career, was doomed to a wasted life and wasted talent; they would take the risk.

They settled her into a very nice stable and resigned themselves to a long wait, for she had to be sedated, operated upon, then be in the recovery box before they could see her. Each with a knot in their stomachs, they waited, visualising a horrible image of their horse upside down in the operating theatre, her throat being cut.

"Oh hell," said Ingrid, "what if it doesn't work?"

"Think positive," replied Lucy, her knuckles white around her coffee cup.

And time went on. Ingrid went to see if there was news and finally, got to see her lovely mare on camera. In the recovery box, already on her feet, still bandaged and padded from the operation, but looking very much a survivor! Ultimately, they found themselves making a huge fuss of her back in the designated stable at the hospital, delighted to find her alert and looking for food.

Two days later, they took her home, all of this having to be juggled around their work somehow! They put her back into a box piled high with clean shavings and later that evening Lucy found her laid down, half asleep, so went and sat with her, savouring the sweetness of the moment and the relief that Alira had come through the operation. She had to have two weeks' box rest and exercising her was taking their lives in their hands, for she had slept off her ordeal and was jumping out of her skin!

Sometimes some grazing in hand would calm her, but not always, so it was a challenge every time. The staples under her jaw were dry and clean, so things were going well so far. The two-day event which Normanton Equestrian Centre held each year took place towards the end of the fortnight of box rest, so she was still confined to her stable, now moody and cross about it.

When finally, the local vet had taken the stitches out, she was allowed to go out in the field and she was crazy, fighting her way out of her head collar, flying off to feel the stretch of her limbs, then bucking that seemed to burst from within and then the inevitable gallop! There was a point where Kentucky bit her on her rump, he must have been thinking, *What is wrong with this mare? She is never still!*

Flaming June came in and it was hot and dry, enabling the recovering patient to go out in the field; Alira maintained fitness well and still looked sleek, was even getting fat. They could lunge her in a head collar now, she was full of energy but they tried to keep her in walk and trot, regularly reporting back to the vet who had done the operation and he was delighted with the mare's progress. Then she started shaking her head a lot, which was alarming, but it turned out to be Papilloma virus in her ears, caused by small black flies that are common, they had crept into her ears and caused wax and plaque. This was not difficult to clear away but she now had to go out in a hood, a mesh hat that fitted over each ear and protected her eyes too. She looked quite kinky in her hood, boots all round, overreach boots on but then no rug, it was so hot.

The weeks passed and Ingrid at last sat on her through one session while Lucy was lunging her, she responded to the rider's legs around her sides while still listening to Lucy's commands. Being lunged every other day she became excellent through all three paces, also was able to extend and steady to command, halt and trot on without hesitation or distraction.

When Ingrid was lunging, the mare would sometimes drop her head and look in at her, as if she was questioning why Ingrid was not on her back! The time would come when she could have her bit in again but it was not yet; a setback occurred where she had an allergic reaction. Her eyes were running, the glands in her neck and throat were enlarged and she was gulping air when exercised. She was prescribed pills and powders and the problems were resolved within about three days. Lucy and Ingrid were suspicious that the spray which was liberally applied to the big arable fields around them had affected her.

Soon after that she was shod, then came in from the field lame on her off fore, so the farrier had to be recalled and the foot tubbed for three days, just as a precaution. But she came right as soon as the shoe was replaced – It had been hammered on a little bit too tightly, an unusual mistake by their farrier.

Lucy and Ingrid were frustrated by all these delays during recovery, impatient to know what would happen when she was back in work with her bridle on and bit in her mouth. However, they kept busy, Ingrid judged at a Preliminary and Novice British Eventing dressage evening, Lucy writing for the judge; their work was demanding too and the weekends enabled a lot of cleaning, polishing and painting while Alira was not in work.

They took her for long walks in hand and she would be proudly stepping out, her beauty unmistakable, turning heads as they went through the nearby village. She would still shy and prance but was not inclined to do more than that and there was no way they were going to lose her.

Chapter 20
The Ultimate Outcome

Dust was blowing across the yard the sun was beginning to illuminate everything with gold and all was quiet; it was still early because Ingrid and Lucy wanted to use the indoor school before anyone was around. The day had at last dawned when Ingrid could ride with bit and bridle. She was using a straight bar 'Happy Mouth' and when she eased herself into the familiar saddle she could hardly bear to pick up the reins. The delicate operation Alira had been subject to had not always solved the problems of the few horses that had it done and Ingrid had read that some went with a head tilt forever after – she would not win any dressage with that!

Ingrid had light hands, but Lucy watched with equal trepidation as her daughter picked up the reins and rode forwards, at first treating the reins as if they were pieces of cotton thread. But as Alira started to mouth the bit and then seek out a contact her rider was able to respond by feeling the reins and gradually establishing a very light contact. Lucy watched with delight as she saw that Alira seemed to have no discomfort, no fear of her mouth and soon her little ears were pricked and she was working properly.

The anxiety about the injury, the weeks of waiting to see if it would heal, the failure of the break to mend by itself, the operation with complete anaesthetic, the long days waiting without riding, all of it was worth it, they had their dressage horse back again! Their beloved Alira was not in any discomfort or danger anymore; as the sun rose and they took her back to the stable to untack there were massive waves of relief flooding through both of them. They hugged each other, patted Alira and could not wait to carry on training her and keep her busy instead of bored. She loved her work and even after all she had been through she put her head down for the bridle and looked for the bit. She never moved away from the saddle as some horses do and showed in her whole demeanour that she felt good about being ridden. Her natural nervousness did not show when she was being trained under saddle. If she showed anxiety or moody mare behaviour it was just necessary for Ingrid to ask her a question, teach her something new, work her a bit harder and she was engaged, attentive, no longer difficult. She was bred to do dressage and that was what she could do; hacking was fraught with dangers and galloping was what happened in the field. Life was good for Alira when she was using her amazing alacrity and ability to move by being trained to do dressage.

The next day, Ingrid rode in searing heat and Alira was her old self, moving without tension and in a rounded outline, working at a higher level than she had ever competed, looking ready to compete again. A couple of lessons with Miranda where horse and rider made maximum effort. But then her work started to be marred by her noisy breathing and she was back to the veterinary hospital to be examined. The verdict being that she had a partially inverted soft palate and because she was not yet fit, working in an outline where her neck was arched and she was taking in a lot of air was a problem. This problem was a feature of Alira's life that occurred whenever she was not fully fit or the atmosphere was dusty and they never could bring themselves to elect to have another operation.

Dull with rain and clouds was the nature of that August, by mid-August Alira was fully fit again and they entered their first competition since February. Ingrid did not ask too much of her and she was a bit over-excited but they were placed in big classes. They went further afield the following week and she travelled well and behaved well, except in the arena!

Her entrance to the arena was impressive, her work was full of panache, her charisma and ability earned her fifth place in a big class. But she threw marks away by rearing when she had to walk four paces and then she also leapt an imaginary chasm that she perceived in one particular part of the arena. Every time she competed at this venue, which was near an old mining town, she would jump this precise part of the arena and Lucy always thought that Alira must sense some instability under the ground.

Consequently, the placing was very satisfying, given her indiscretions!

Autumn approached and another competition was lost because she broke into canter twice, ebullient and enthusiastic, but they would not have had her any other way. Each time they studied what was correct and what needed improvement, then at home her schooling would be exact and fantastic. But the atmosphere of competition just made horse and rider feel that little bit different and she was such a sensitive horse, the slightest difference increased tension and she would get strong and opinionated – convinced she knew better than her rider what should come next!

With such a clever horse, it was inadvisable to practise actual tests, because she may ruin it by anticipating the next movement and they did many different tests, always on the basis of correct schooling and the scales of training, freedom, fluency, contact, impulsion from behind.

Chapter 21
More Slings and Arrows

The sky was arrayed in gorgeous pink and blue as the sun rose behind the stables. Ingrid had got her mare ready to go out in the field; she got up at five o'clock every morning to complete the stables routine before driving to work, so she would rise, wash, dress in her stables gear and drive the two or three miles to the yard. Alira would be whinnying as soon as she heard the car engine, dropping her voice to a low, soft sound as Ingrid approached and then sounding more urgent once she had welcomed her, emphasising that she was hungry. Therefore, the first task had to be short keep in a bucket, then Ingrid would go to get hay, which had to be shaken up to free it from dust, stuffed into a net which was then tied carefully in the stable with a quick-release knot. A brush over her sleek coat, the shavings brushed out of her tail, then Ingrid would start the mucking out while Alira had a brief munch on her hay. When Alex was ready with Kentucky, Ingrid would take her horse out to the field with him and the two horses would be turned out into the field to graze together, Alex and Ingrid would go back to the stable block and finish the mucking out, so that there were clean stables ready for when the horses came in.

This specific morning, Alira was ready first and outside in the yard waiting for Alex to bring Kentucky – when he did, Alex had to pop back to his stable for some reason and asked Ingrid to hold Kentucky. She was holding Alira beside her in her right hand and Kentucky beside her in her left, as she had done multiple times before, in fact she sometimes brought both of them in from the field, leading them side by side. Both horses were stood quietly, ears pricked, looking towards their field.

Sometimes, things happen quickly and nothing anyone can do will obviate disaster. Suddenly, Ingrid saw Kentucky's head snake in front of her towards Alira, a flash of bared teeth and then he had bitten the mare's nose, a spurt of bright red blood from Alira as she shrieked in pain, then a mess, blood everywhere, the mare in a panic, Ingrid shouting for Alex to get Kentucky, a darkening pool of blood on the concrete. Struggling to hold Alira, who was running backwards, blood still pouring from her nose, a rip by her nostril, deep, serious. Ingrid distraught, a million questions in her head, why? Why now? Why had the big horse decided to attack his field mate, out of the blue and so viciously? She was using all her resources to calm her mare, terrified of what she would see when she looked more closely, but getting her to stand still, frightened as Alira dropped her head and stood dejected, the blood still dripping. Stroking her neck, talking to her, trying to sound as reassuring as possible when all she felt was panic; but it worked and the enormous trust that Alira had in her meant that she could get her safely back into her stable, ring Lucy, ring the vet.

Alex's insouciance did not help. He had taken Kentucky out to the field as if nothing had happened. With her psychologist's head, Ingrid told herself that he was frightened of his responsibility for what his horse had done. But in her heart she felt furious, mutinous, enraged, appalled, a whole mix of vertiginous emotions that culminated in a sick feeling of dread when the vet voiced a concern that if Alira lost her nostril then there are major concerns about the horse working again. For horses rely on a huge intake of air that their flared nostrils allow them to take in to their large lungs to enervate their immense proportion of muscle.

She spoke to Lucy then and tears came. It seemed so recently that Alira's body had to heal a great cut in her throat. Often, Lucy could instil calm in her daughter, but this time it was difficult, especially because the clock was ticking; they were both supposed to be at work! The vet had dealt with cleansing and treating the wound, given Alira injections, promised to return tomorrow, the bleeding had stopped at last; it was hard to leave the injured animal, but needs must, so Ingrid gave her a great, deep bed, plenty of hay to pick at and left for a late arrival at work. She normally went back to her flat to get changed and was never late, she considered missing that out this morning, but then realised she was spattered with blood, so raced home and quickly changed.

"How is this fair? Damn that horse, damn Alex, to hell with everything!" She railed against this turn of fate, she harangued the man who did not seem to care, she wished she could turn the clock back and stop this morning's events from happening. She was angry with Kentucky but knew he was just a horse, it had just happened and they would never know why.

Arriving at work, she already felt exhausted, but soon the demands of caring for children's futures and trying to solve the problems which they were experiencing within education meant that she could not dwell on the latest turn of events with her ill-fated horse. When she found herself back at the yard that evening, it was to find Lucy assessing the state of Alira's nose.

"Well, it looks pretty ghastly, but we know she heals well and we know how to care for skin damage!" Lucy concluded.

Ingrid's mind flitted feverishly over the eye that Alira could have lost, the operation that had left her full of staples and the vet's ominous words about losing her nostril. She told Lucy the vet's warning but Lucy was pragmatic.

"Hopefully we can stop that from happening. The main thing is that we avoid infection, if we can stop it from going septic, it will heal."

Consequently, there followed a regime of utmost cleanliness and gentle discouragement of anyone touching her near the wound on her nose.

Mixing a feed that had so many powders in it that it no longer looked palatable, Lucy was worried about the amount of antibiotics their mare had already had in her life, but then thought, *Needs must, I so hope she is not scarred too badly.*

The following day, they kept her in, but the next day she was fretting so she went out for half a day. Four days after the bite, Ingrid went into the stable in the morning and immediately thought, *Oh my god, what is that smell?*

She thought it was somewhere between a very old dead rat and a horribly blocked drain, but then realised to her dismay that it was Alira's nose. Around the bite, it was swollen and the raw area was covered in a thick, greenish pus; this is what reeked. Ingrid bathed her with salt water and the pus kept coming, thick and revolting, eventually, she resorted to a small syringe to get right into the deep part of the wound and clean it all out.

I should have been a vet, she thought.

The mare had to stay in then for days, until the wound scabbed over; it took even more antibiotics to reduce the festering mucus that the centre of her injury produced. Days of washing with saline solution and finally it scabbed over; turning her out into the field they were terrified that she would knock the scab off, but she was just on her own in a little square of field behind electric fence, with Kentucky nearby. She seemed to have no particular fear of him, but they dared not risk putting them in together and of course, there was the negotiating task of knowing when Kentucky was going to be brought in, not to leave her on her own.

Alex seemed to have relaxed around them somewhat. He tried to be helpful, but Ingrid still felt that he was not regretful about what had happened and he should have been. Lucy reflected that, "He should be paying the vet bills really, but I am not going to try and make him to do that, so he could at least say he was sorry. I am starting to have an aversion to him; I wish we did not have to rely on him turning out his horse to be able to turn out ours."

"Yes," agreed Ingrid, "what we need is a companion pony for her, just a nice quiet pony who can go out with her and keep her calm."

Incredibly, three weeks later, she was back on form again and the flesh that had been ripped apart was healing together and had formed a small volcano shape above her nostril, which had regained its normal definition. The lump was proud flesh that had formed in the middle of the bite and never did go away completely, but it did eventually grow hair over it and was not noticeable with a casual glance.

Alira did not even become head-shy; she seemed to know that all the administrations to her nose were to help her, just as she had when her eye was injured. She became, if anything, more devoted to her owners and thrilled by their presence but started acting more like a horse and less like a pet when she started work again, soon competing again and smashing the opposition. The first venue was to the South of Normanton, well down the motorway, where she got a first and a second in Novice

Affiliated classes, scores well up into the seventies. Waves of relief flooded over Lucy and Ingrid, it seemed no harm, only delay, had happened to her dressage career.

A few nights later, Lucy watched a skein of geese fly noisily over the premises that belonged to Miranda. Ingrid was mounted and warming up slowly; the sky was coloured with clouds that reflected the setting sun of a pleasant but cool autumn day. The lesson progressed and Lucy filmed this time. Both horse and rider looked fit and primed for action. Miranda put them through their paces and Ingrid sat deep as she performed a leg-yield right across the school, sat back as the mare crossed the school from corner to corner in medium trot, powering forward as the leg aids requested and the hands allowed. Then into a joyous canter, light on the bit, controlled but flowing – a loop from the track perfectly executed – Ingrid extended the canter then brought the little horse back to a collected canter, the horse's low hocks enabling her mare to sit her weight back onto her hocks and Ingrid could contain her power. She came back with a seamless transition to trot and then to do shoulder-in down the long side, Alira's neck arched and curved inward, her forelegs meeting the ground just off the track while her hind legs remained on the track, going forward with exuberance but no disobedience.

Miranda enthused when they had finished. She could be cutting, even cruel, although always good humoured, but now she raved, "She is working at Medium level now; you are going to have no trouble moving up a level!"

Ingrid always doubted herself and it seemed that she hardly believed her, but Lucy knew the pair of them had it in them to go a long way. They drove back happily chatting, Alira switching one ear back to listen to them through the little window between the cab and her stall in the horsebox, seeing a fox out on an early expedition to get his supper.

The next competition saw them go to a venue where the dressage arenas were outdoors and quite exposed; Alira was nervous but therefore listened closely to her rider's aids, she won both classes and attracted much admiration. The next four classes saw Alira placed second in all, just missing the top accolade by getting too excited after canter and consequently not settling to her walk. She was getting too exhilarated when out in the field as well; her portion of field was fenced off with electric tape and she had galloped through the tape one day, snapping ropes and posts and narrowly escaping injury. She lost a shoe was all, very lucky compared to what could have happened to her. Lucy complained that she did not like electric tape for horses, but if they put Alira into a big space, she was too nervous and could achieve too much speed when she galloped. Being schooled for dressage, she could gallop even in a tiny space but was less likely to get too wild. When her area was moved to part of the field which included a hill, she played on it for a long time and inflamed her near side foreleg, which meant giving her a week of rest. The weather was now unpredictable as November brought its chill and Alira caught cold going back into work, sweating hard during a lesson with Miranda and then not getting cooled down enough before going out in the field. Her two owners berated themselves over this mistake, missing a competition as a consequence.

There was a sudden and massive reaction from Alira in the next test that she competed in; at the end of a nearly perfect performance she refused to go in the right direction, leapt, bucked, half reared, then agreed to trot down the centre line for Ingrid to salute the judges. No prizes for her that day!

There was some reason for such a sudden misdemeanour and they could only speculate what. The next competition followed soon after. It was Alira's favourite venue, so they had entered two classes and she behaved beautifully to win the first one, but Ingrid sensed something was wrong. There was a downhill slope to the warm-up arena and when Lucy led her down it she was alerted to a slight hesitation in her step. Ingrid agreed that it might be a stiff back and they withdrew from the second class, took her home and soon after, had her back treated by a reputable horse physiotherapist. The battle to keep their horse happy and in work continued!

Chapter 22
Calm in the Field

"*What* is his name?" Yvonne shrieked.

"Mervyn," replied Ingrid firmly. "You cannot call him that! You can't have Alira Compliquer and 'Mervyn'!"

"Yes, I can," responded Ingrid, grinning. "Don't laugh at his name!"

She hugged his neck and Mervyn just carried on plodding across the yard. The little pony was footsore when not on grass, but seemed indifferent to what happened to him, life was to be endured.

Mervyn came into their lives like a saviour; small, solid and white, unimpressed by the hubris of Alira in the field, stoic, the most important aspect of life to him was eating. Lucy and Ingrid saw him advertised in the local paper and went to see him, up in the hills of the North East. He was a grey Welsh Section C, so about 13.1 hands high and so old he had gone white, but still life in him! The little fellow had spent his life in a riding school, being ridden by loads of kids, labouring under the mixed fortunes of being a pretty pony with an honest work ethic, so had been in high demand; therefore, was driven long and hard to get his Haylage – the only feed he got, out of a circular feeder in a field where he competed with about twenty other ponies. Thus, he was fiercely defensive about his food, would squeal, strike and whip round to kick anyone who ventured near when he was eating. The people who were advertising him now had bought him cheaply from the riding school for their teenage daughter, who had quickly lost interest in him, preferring boys to ponies! For this reason, he had been foundering in a field for a year or two, neglected because the family did not really know one end of a horse from the other.

Lucy and Ingrid handled him gently as they inspected him, finding two years of coat grown into itself beneath his long, tangled mane and tail. *Healthy enough*, thought Lucy, *although needing some attention*, for he had ergots at the back of his fetlocks that had grown almost to the ground. These hard, bony protuberances are not usually a problem, but in an old pony they can become overt and grow too far. Ingrid had mentioned that he would need the farrier when she picked up his feet, so they would ask their farrier to trim them if they bought him. The risk of this process is profuse bleeding if they are trimmed too short, so they knew it to be best to get an experienced person to do it. Mervyn was a risk worth taking and he had his name from where he had been bred in the Welsh Mountains, a little village amongst some hills called The Rivals, where Lucy's mum, Ingrid's grandmother, had first ridden ponies when evacuated away from her home during wartime. She would often wax lyrical about the wonderful riding she had, setting out from Merfyn to wander the Welsh hills. Parting with a few hundred pounds to have Mervyn to keep their mare calm in the field did not seem too much, as he would probably save them that in the vet bills that they would avoid having to pay for Alira's minor injuries!

Two days later, they drove the horsebox to collect Mervyn and brought him back to Normanton. Now, of course, there would be more livery bills to pay, but they made a deal with Anita that she could use him for the riding school which she had just set up, as long as it was purely for little children on the leading rein, only in walk and trot, in return for a reduced livery bill. This arrangement meant that Mervyn had a pen in a big barn adjoined to the small indoor school so that he was available for them to use him 'occasionally'. His main, priority job was to accompany Alira whilst she was in the field, so he went out when she did and came in when she did. She was soon quite enamoured with him and took great reassurance from his stolid presence, going to the field quietly, grazing steadily through the day and coming in, impatient to get past her smaller, slower friend, but pleased with herself and relaxed about her life.

Mervyn began to look a bonny lad with Lucy's solicitous attention. His tangled tail was brushed out, his mane combed neatly to one side and slowly she was removing two years or more of coat, ending up covered in white hair herself! Then

Ingrid and she became aware that all was not as they had agreed; they kept seeing big children on Mervyn, not on a leading rein, going around the arena, booting Mervyn into a canter with the encouragement of the instructor, then bouncing around on his back, even though they were clearly too heavy for him.

Furious, Lucy went to find Anita, unsuccessfully; but did see that Anita had put a horse in the pen next to Mervyn and it was easily able to reach over and eat his hay. She spoke to Anita's daughter to say that it must be moved, the pony was getting extremely angry about this big horse eating his precious food and it was not fair, they were designated pony pens and should not have horses in.

The following night was dark and cold. Lucy and Ingrid were by Alira's stable finishing off for the evening when there was a shout, from the top of the yard, to come quickly. Ingrid raced off and Lucy followed; she saw Ingrid vault the five-bar gate into Mervyn's pen and a young girl was looking on anxiously.

"I think he might have hurt himself, his leg was stuck between the bars," she told Lucy.

Ingrid was looking very serious. "It's bad," she said.

Mervyn had been kicking out at the big horse – which was still there – and let fly with both hind legs, one of which had gone through the planking and he was now bleeding profusely, for he had pulled skin off as he pulled it out. Getting him out of the pen, they realised it was more than superficial; the actual bone of the hock was exposed and he could not put the leg down, it hung at a peculiar angle.

"This does not look good," Lucy voiced the fears they both had and she proceeded to ring the vet.

It was late and dark and it would be classed as an emergency call, therefore would be expensive but needs must. The vet would be there 'As soon as possible'.

Lucy held Mervyn and tried to distract him for he was trembling and sweating with the pain; she talked to him, scratched him and stroked him. Lucy and Ingrid felt infuriated, because if the horse had not been there in the next pen, stealing Mervyn's hay, this would never have happened, but they also felt compassion for poor Mervyn, bleeding and in pain.

When at last the vet arrived, she expertly cleansed the wound, having given Mervyn an immediate shot of painkiller and an antibiotic injection. She then had her fingers inside the wound exploring the damage causing Ingrid to feel mildly sick. The vet looked grave.

"He has broken the leg at the hock joint, I'm afraid, you will need to think what you want to do."

They knew the implications of her words; put him down or keep him. A long healing process to go through and then? The response to Lucy's question about whether he would become sound again, was negative, probably not. The vet was there for two hours, dressing the wound and bandaging his leg tightly to prevent the joint from moving.

That night they thanked the vet very much, put a huge bed in his pen – the horse had gone, but Anita had appeared and abruptly said that he now could have a stable next to Alira's, he could not stay there in the pens with the riding school ponies. Not now as he was no use to her anymore, was the inference. She had at least said he could have a stable near their horse, but it did mean he would incur the full cost of livery. They put his rugs on and went home, tired and disconsolate, to lie awake and stew over this latest turn of events.

The morning after was bleak and bitterly cold with a dusting of snow on the yard, when Ingrid went to try and move him from his pen to the new stable he was to have. She had made up her mind, that if he could not make it across the yard, they would have to take that most awful of decisions and call the vet back to him to end his struggle.

Her hopes were lifted when he looked alert and ate his breakfast; after which she got Yvonne to come and help her and proceeded to coach him across the yard on three legs. Mervyn was a tough guy. Ingrid was moved by his courage and bravery. It was as if he thought, *You saved my life last night so I will go anywhere with you now* and balanced by a woman on either side of him he made it to his new stable.

After showing such fortitude, Ingrid could only think that he deserved to be given a chance. "We're keeping him," she told Lucy later, on the phone driving to work. "He is such a brave boy! He is in his new place tucking into some hay, with a massive bed, looking happy to be alive!"

Lucy was delighted for the little fellow but could not help but think about the vet bills; he was not insured and that leg would need dressing and bandaging every week. The bandaging inevitably had to go from his stifle to his fetlock, so was substantial – and what about his job of keeping Alira company?

That night at the yard, both women were perusing his bandaging and Ingrid had an answer to that issue. "Mervyn is a Welsh pony, he will not be happy kept in all the time and anyway, as you say, he needs to do his job. He will have to go out with her and I will cover his bandaging with cling film and then secure it with duct tape; that should keep it dry and clean."

Lucy thought that Mervyn was not the only one showing fortitude and valour. He and Ingrid were bound to conquer this latest challenge!

Chapter 23
Mervyn Beats the Odds

The vet was surprised by their decision to keep him when she came the day after. Rarely is it seen as viable to try and nurse a horse with a broken leg. Horses move all the time and are unlikely to recover their soundness. In other words, they end up as lame animals; the vet bills are huge and in Mervyn's case there was a wound to heal as well, a very deep and nasty wound. Ingrid was keen to care for him and asked if she could be shown how to clean and dress the wound herself, to save some of the expense. She had after all had experience of equine wound care! The vet demonstrated and agreed to come again the following day to watch Ingrid do the same process. It had to be a very firm bandage to both hold the dressing in place and support the broken leg, with packing in the hollow by the hock. There began a long two months of veterinary procedures for Ingrid, where she redressed the wound and replaced the bandages repeatedly and after the first week took him out with Alira; on his leg a layer of surgical wrap, a soft bandage, then rolls of vet wrap in varying colours! This all protected by cling film from stifle to hoof, then duct tape likewise, with no gaps anywhere to let in any water or mud.

Mervyn was anxious about these processes at first, because cleaning the wound was painful for him, but he was also relishing his life of ease and exceptional individual attention – something he had never had and which he thought to be an excellent privilege. After various sessions of wound dressing where Lucy held his head, he realised that this was for his benefit and Ingrid could do it herself each morning before work, although she had a day off on the weekend when Lucy did it. When he could put his toe down he did and then developed an awkward gait, but it got him along and he was happy to get to the field and graze.

Alira was pleased to have her stoic little friend back, although she could not understand why he was not interested when she gave the signal: "Come on, let's gallop!" And she just had to canter a circle round him and then she would continue her eating.

Spring came, the weather was mild and the inevitable happened; he got sweaty and itchy underneath the bandage and had to be treated for infection, with antibiotic powders and pain killer. Finally, the bandage could be left off and a cream applied to reduce the proud flesh that was forming. The wound was healing, but there was going to be a big scar down the inside of his off hind leg. The hock joint did not bend, so he had to move with a dishing action; but move he did and four months after his accident he did have a little canter in the field with Alira, glad to feel the warmth of spring on his body and to have sweet new grass that was bursting through. Because he could do no work, he had to be monitored closely for getting too fat and now another danger; flies came and opened the wound a tad, for which problem Lucy resorted to an old remedy, a spot of Stockholm Tar, which worked a treat. A large scab formed next and so regular bathing was needed to soften it and the vet prescribed more gel to heal, soothe and prevent overgrowth of the new flesh which was forming.

Five months after the injury, he was signed off by the vet and Lucy offered to pay the bill, because Ingrid had initially paid for Mervyn. The vet bill came to more than the original cost of the pony, so Lucy decided that she was now a joint owner, just like she was with Alira! The regime of care had not ended yet however. With the approaching summer, it was necessary to wash the leg in saltwater when he came in from the field, to cleanse and heal, then as the scab reduced, to clean the area with gauze and surgical spirit which finally brought off the last scab, with the help of a little wound powder. Hence, by the middle of the summer his leg was healed, although still showing a long scar down the inside of his hind leg. They knew he was better when, having turned him out into the field with Alira, he had a canter and a buck and a kick with her! What a brave pony! Mervyn would always move with a stiff hind leg but now was always lively, a different pony from the one they had bought. Mervyn seemed to know that he was special and valued now, he had a wiser, kinder eye and an enthusiasm for life that was absent when they first owned him. He lived in honourable retirement now, his sole purpose being a companion for Alira, nobody rode him unless Lucy's little grandson sat on – very briefly, because the little boy was more interested in things with wheels and flashing lights than ponies! The horse-loving gene seemed to be absent in Sophie's child.

Mervyn helped Alira too, for the last interruption to her training was diagnosed as a lumbar spasm and she had to rest but could be out in the field; clearly, galloping would not be advantageous so they were glad that she settled for the prescribed six weeks and was spending her time grazing alongside Mervyn. The owners of the livery stables had seen fit to start excavating behind Alira's stable, with no warning and without thought for the mare inside. She had been circling the small box and twisted a shoe off, luckily not standing on a nail this time. This was the sort of infuriating thing that happened from time to time and with the totally preventable accident that had happened to Mervyn, they could not help but think they were resented in some way, or perhaps just not considered.

Chapter 24
Another New Year Dawns

The patchy remains of a moderate snowfall laid around the yard at Normanton, time was spent every morning gritting the path to Alira's stable and thawing out taps with boiling water, the horse worked regularly in the school and was coming back to fitness. Then she started to challenge her rider every step of the way, so schooling sessions were high intensity, producing lovely work after a battle to get her to become light on the bit, to settle and to listen to the aids. Soon, they were at a competition again, but the usual round of winter colds and flu had affected her rider this time, and after a poor performance in the Preliminary class, she withdrew from the Novice and they went home. Rising nine years old now, she was supremely agile and able to exploit any time that her rider was not keeping her busy.

Lucy tried to understand Alira's mind and wondered if she needed a change of task, so she taught her to jump, on the lunge. There was barely any teaching needed to be done, for she quickly understood what was required of her and loved this new game. She was and always had been, eminently forward going, so placing a couple of poles in her way; she just took them in her stride. When the jumps got bigger, she made a lovely parabola over them, but got very hot and excited. This meant limiting the time spent jumping, which seemed to have made her more strong and temperamental under saddle, she was starting to object to being asked to do dressage!

Ingrid was daunted by this new desire to rush, to argue with her and to run back. She entered into a clinic that was run for a day at Normanton, where entrants could pick their own dressage test and have feedback from the judge. Ingrid chose Novice 39 and knew she was up against her mare's temperament as soon as she entered the arena. Alira was looking about. Everything was spooky, she was in season and her sides were hard and unresponsive to the leg, she was against the hand. Ingrid was determined that she was going to do this test and her horse was going to have to listen to her. The test took a long time as Ingrid overcame every challenge that Alira threw at her. She sat tight, calm and deep and quietly insisted on each and every movement, defying the misbehaviour of her mare. Alira reared, she bounced through the canter circles, she ran back into the wall, in one corner she ran back into the wall, got stuck in her own defiance, stood up and finally came down onto her forelegs!

Eventually, she completed the test! Her neck was arched and her head high as she came up the centre line, she was flecked with froth from the bit, sweating and looked amazing. Ingrid was triumphant because she had overcome every argument, but the test had taken a long, long time because of Alira's arguments! The judge stepped out of his car and said, "He needs to be trained again, go back to the basics and start again."

Lucy and Ingrid laughed, perfectly aware of how it must have looked to the judge and amused that he must have thought Alira was male – maybe even a stallion!

They had no chance of going back to the beginning, for Alira was qualified for Regional Finals again and having missed two of these events due to her enforced rest they set out to Rowallan, way up in Scotland, for a regional final that would bring her up against many very good horses. Alira would never again misbehave in a test in quite the way she did during that Novice 39 at Normanton, it was as if she agreed that she would obey her rider – well, *most* of the time! She was fit and explosive, but actually was very well behaved after the long journey up to Scotland, when they led her out of the horsebox she appeared to be amazed at the space around her but reassured by the presence of many of her colleagues, other horses who seemed mostly to be calm and experienced at their job. Lucy led her around and she was interested in everything but did not play up as long as they were reasonably close to the buildings and horseboxes. The big, wild moor out there was threatening and not the place for Alira to get loose!

Ingrid had found where their horse was to be stabled and Alira bravely strode down the corridor between lots of horses and they found her stable to be on the end of the block and to her approval, for she immediately got down and rolled in the nice pile of shavings which Ingrid had put in. The situation of her stable meant that it was easy for Lucy and Ingrid to pop into the huge main arena and watch some competitors doing their tests, then quickly go to attend to their horse's needs. Her class was taking place the next morning and that evening, after another walk out, they left her to go to their accommodation, working out that they had plenty of time to get everything prepared prior to her class the following day.

The next day, after Alira had been fed, mucked out, groomed, her mane plaited and tack placed upon her, Ingrid rode her into the warm up arena with a careful plan in her head to get her ready for the Regional Final. Somehow, the time had slipped by and Lucy said, "You've only ten minutes to warm up, hurry on with it!"

Ingrid realised to her horror that Lucy was right and did what she could in an abbreviated stretch of time, before she was called into the huge arena with huge flags from many countries hanging down above them. Suddenly feeling a rush of nerves, Ingrid felt her chest tighten and mind go numb, then told herself to take her time, walk round until she calmed down, told herself to be calm for Alira's sake, reflected that the surface was perfect. Then she trotted on and the bell went for her to enter the dressage boards. Alira was aware this was something important and went beautifully, while Lucy watched with a knot in her stomach, wishing that she drank so that she could have had a swift drink to calm herself! She knew that Ingrid was not confident that her mare would complete the test calmly and her mother agonised for her, knowing that her ambition was to win and that her horse had the ability to do just that.

Each movement was stylish and accurate. Horse and rider showing unity and harmony, the mare demonstrating that she was supple, fluent, light on the contact, working from behind and doing all the things she was supposed to do. The test was almost finished when they turned up the centre line to walk up towards the judges as was required in this test. Alira thought no! I like to trot up the middle and try as Ingrid might, to get her to walk and walk straight; her mount jogged sideways up that magnificent arena and lost her chance of ribbons and adulation. Ingrid had saluted the judges and could not dwell on what had just happened because she felt as if Alira was about to take off in a gallop to leave the arena and it took all her strength and firmness to prevent that happening.

No prize giving for them, but it had still been an honour to take part and a good experience for all of them; Alira had by no means disgraced herself and they had time to have a look around once she was back in her stable. Coffee and cake while someone strummed a guitar energised them for the journey back home, so Alira was loaded and Ingrid drove out of the Equestrian centre, taking her turn at driving because Lucy had driven on the way up. Alira travelled well until they had to stop at a service station to visit the toilets. The horse in the back was suddenly rocking the waggon, the thuds and bangs suggested some wild, unbroken youngster, yet when Lucy looked in at her she was fine, just absolutely furious! She took exception to that service station and the minute they drove away became completely calm and sensible again! Whether it reminded her of that first, long journey when they stopped on their way home and the young Alira was so stressed, they would never know.

Rowallan had been an uplifting experience for Alira and she was back to her old self; the next competition saw her winning the Trailblazers qualifier with a score of 72%, after which a routine check of her back caused the physiotherapist to comment that very few horses were as supple and comfortable as Alira.

However, life never stayed on the level where Alira was concerned, because things kept happening to her. The next minor incident was when she got her rug stuck in the fence while leaning over to reach some tasty vegetation, then in a panic, pulled back to get free and hurt herself as her hind feet slipped beneath her. Nothing that could not be put right with a bit more physio! The cost of Alira was something that Lucy monitored and regularly divided between herself and Ingrid at the end of each month, but she never dared to add up the accumulated cost!

Another near disaster occurred, perhaps instigated by Alira's season, which seemed to progressively make her more hormonal. But she and Mervyn were innocent and oblivious to danger until Kentucky jumped into their field, tried to kill Mervyn and chased Alira. He was the sort of gelding that still has some stallion traits, usually hidden behind his well-trained obedience, but Alira had an effect on him which he did not understand, so he became unreasonably aggressive.

Thankfully, Ingrid was there preparing evening stables and saw the drama unfolding; one minute seeing her horses grazing in the spring sunshine then the big chestnut horse with teeth bared was trying to bite Mervyn, who manfully stood up to him, rearing up and striking out while squealing and trying to be as threatening as possible.

The big horse grabbed the top of Mervyn's mane and tried to shake him, but Mervyn got free when Ingrid came racing into the field and shouted at Kentucky, "Get back, get off!"

Kentucky shot away and turned his attention to Alira, galloping at her with a horrid face, ears flat back, mouth open and teeth bared – Alira fled and he was after her. Fleet of foot and agile, Alira evaded him time after time as they circled the field, but soon he closed upon her and Ingrid in desperation opened the gate, calling her horse urgently, "Come here, girl, Alira, come on, lass!"

She saw her mare spot the gate, then the galloping horse swerved and shot through it in a burst of speed that was astronomical; Ingrid slammed it before Kentucky could follow. Alira stopped, her sides heaving, her eye wild. Ingrid grabbed her and led her into the stable, rushing back to save Mervyn; but with the departure of Alira, Kentucky had slowed and become calm. Ingrid was able to catch him and put him back into his field.

Amazingly, this extraordinary occurrence did not seem to have done any harm to horse or pony, but the next thing was Saharan sand! The southerly winds brought the remnants of a dust storm from the deserts of Sahara, which did not affect all horses as badly as it did Alira, but she was sensitive to so many things! Her head swelled and her glands became enlarged. When ridden, she appeared flat, without her usual presence and charisma and her wind was not good, very noisy when she worked in an outline. But with some anti-histamine, this passed and she carried on winning first and second prizes, until she went slightly lame on her near fore.

After a week of rest and painkiller, she was animated again but unsettled in her stable and was a crazy hoodlum in her field. There was always this conflict that when she was unsound. Rest was the logical antidote, but Alira being full of fire and energy would build up so much vigour and verve that she was difficult to manage and a danger to herself in the field. Then back under saddle, she was strong, pushy, seemed too fit, even though her feed had been cut down to the minimum; but she settled with a lot of patience and persistence.

The excavation behind her stable had been to make a foundation for the muck-heap, which given that there were some twenty horses there, got fairly big and was making Alira's stable too hot. Consequently, they swopped Mervyn's stable with hers, as Mervyn would not become agitated by the heat in the way that his Warmblood friend did. The move at first made her wild and disorientated, so that her usual good stable manners went out of the window and caused an accident that would not normally have happened. She was tied up in the stable and Lucy was grooming her, when she suddenly swung her quarters sideways. Lucy was by her near hind leg and the offside hind hoof came across and incongruously, stood on Lucy's boot, pinning her down so that the mare's quarters slammed against her and flung her down, knocking her head on the floor and jarring all those joints that caused her a lot of pain any way. She yelled for Ingrid to come and her daughter was there in a flash, helping her up from the smelly floor where she had just swept up the horse pee, getting the shavings out of her hair.

Unfortunately, it was just after that when Ingrid and her partner went on holiday, so James and Lucy were left in charge. James helped with mucking out and water carrying, while Lucy tried to keep the mare calm and interested, taking her out to be led in hand around the yard or lunging her in the school. The night before they were due back, Lucy took her down the back lane to a nearby village. Alira's behaviour initially was exemplary, she coped with some cattle in a field and a bicycle, so Lucy was decidedly pleased with her and let her graze on the verge at the bottom of the lane – their field was fairly bare now and her horse relished the bit of grass. This was Alira; so of course, the unusual and unexpected had to occur, just to send her past her usual state of calm and into a frenzy of fear and horror.

The June day was lovely and calm, evening was approaching and farm tractors were going home. She was okay with them, a quiet pat as they came past and a soothing word was all it took to reassure her. But then, behind a tall hedge, something began to appear, accompanied by a hissing and whooshing sound; it was brightly coloured and as it came jerkily into view it was growing bigger all the time. Somebody was blowing up a bouncy castle for their kids, but it is hard to imagine a scenario more terrifying to a horse; with Alira, if she could understand it, then all well and good, but this, this was beyond comprehension.

The mare flew round in a circle, her head was up, white showing in her eyes, her nostrils flared – and then that snort! A piercing high pitched, shrill blast of air down her nose, a warning: *I cannot tolerate this, I have to go!*

Lucy had the bridle on her so managed to hang on and set off to take her home, but Alira wanted to bolt home. Lucy had to stop her, for a bolting horse on the lane could be highly dangerous, not to mention galloping into the yard at speed. That was, if she did not come down on rough terrain or on the turn into the yard. Twisting the reins so that she could hold close to the bit, she pulled Alira's head round towards her and forced her elbow into the horse's neck. Wrestled her all the way home like that until finally she could clip on the lunge rein inside the indoor school and allow her to let off steam, which she did big style, bucking and kicking as she flew round, releasing some of that adrenaline which had built up. Finally putting her back in her stable, Lucy felt battered and aching. She had used every ounce of strength, but she had not let go of her. Crazy horse, but what were the odds against somebody blowing up a bouncy castle behind an adjacent hedge? She had to laugh, it happened so many times that the bizarre and improbable happened to her and Alira.

Previously, there was a time when Lucy had walked her down the very quiet lane the opposite way, having some trouble passing the field with a herd of horses in, but that had not been too difficult; further on, they could walk down to the end of the lane and she could let Alira have a few mouthfuls of grass. Something then galvanised her horse into panic mode: there was a man up at the top of a very tall ash tree, about to cut off a branch. Alira was filled with horror at something so disturbing and inexplicable to her, so a similar battle had to be undertaken to get her back home, exacerbated by the horses in the field also being afraid and massing into a herd, which then came galloping past.

How Lucy did not lose her she had no idea, she just seemed to possess super human strength where her horse was concerned, but then paid the price of aching muscles afterwards.

Chapter 25
She's a Star!

Driving the horsebox towards the motorway, their mare content in the back, Ingrid in charge this time, Lucy with her feet up in the passenger seat, they were in high spirits.

"I cannot believe it is a year since we went to Trailblazers!" exclaimed Ingrid.

"I know, it's brilliant to be going again and this time she's qualified for two classes!" replied Lucy. "It should be great fun; at least we know what we are doing this time a bit more."

Lucy watched swifts arcing through the sky and then zooming towards earth; the blue sky seemed to predict that the weather was going to be kind to them and they had everything they needed stored in the horsebox. This included their suitcases behind the seats, her hay and feed in the back, tack in the tack locker, bandages and boots in the overhead locker alongside two first aid kits, equine and human. They soon reached the motorway and made good progress. Alira riding in the back like a professional traveller – she loved smooth roads!

They stopped halfway to pour water out of a big drum and give her a drink. She was very warm as the sun got up so Ingrid opened another window. When they finally got to the National Showground, there was a buzz of excitement about the place. Alira's head was up, looking out of her back window, as they crossed the small bridge and were waved into a position to park their box. Alira paused at the top of the ramp as she was unloaded, with raised head and pricked ears, surveying the proceedings, then she came quietly down the ramp and walked around with Lucy, who then took her to her allocated stable.

Ingrid had bought two bags of shavings to add to what was already in the box, so the mare was in there and rolled, before getting to know her neighbours on either side. Lucy was a bit worried that one of them was going to bite her because he was a big horse of Warmblood type, but his owners appeared and he was soon distracted by being groomed and sorted out. His owners assured them that he would not bite and he never did. They could not forget Kentucky's savage bite and Alira forever afterwards had a bump above her left nostril, the remnants of that fateful day. Thanks to Aloe Vera gel, it was covered with hair and not easily noticeable, but they certainly never wanted anything like that to happen again!

They left Alira to go and have a look around. The warm-up arena already busy with people schooling horses in preparation for tomorrow, or just exercising them. The colourful flags blowing in the breeze, the tents for VIP's and one where competitors went to collect numbers and some selling horse kit, the food tent already disseminating smells of bacon and chips. More people were buying ice cream than hot food, for the heat of the day was mounting, which sent Alira's owners back to the stable to take her rug off.

Later that evening, Lucy took her for a walk down by the river, where it was cool, but soon regretted it because clegs were down there in abundance and soon started to bite Alira. They retreated up the hill where the breeze blew them away but made sure she had plenty of fly spray on when they had finished stable chores for the night.

This year they stayed in slightly up-market digs and enjoyed a pleasant evening meal, after they had finally got the horsebox parked! The next day dawned with a beautiful sunrise, cool and misty but promising heat later on. Alira greeted them with a deep whinny and tucked into her breakfast. There was evidence of her being laid down asleep, so she had been relaxed in her wooden and canvas stable. Much attention followed to get her clean, shining and plaited, rewarded by a lot of admiration from the other people around them. When Ingrid was mounted, Lucy followed down to the warm-up arena, which really represented a challenge for Alira as it was extremely busy. The mare was daunted as she went in and shrunk a little, as big horses cantered by in both directions, but her rider's still, calm seat and kind hands steadied her and soon she was listening to the aids which Ingrid gave to her and started to work properly.

Canter work was the most difficult because Ingrid was worried that she would be explosive or onward going, risking coming into a too close proximity to other horses. Alira had got over her fear of being kicked, but sometimes a big horse reminiscent of Prince, especially if it was high blown so breathed loudly, would spook her and she would lose her rhythm.

"You have to go and wait to go in," called Lucy.

Ingrid rode up to her and halted for her to remove Alira's bandages.

"Good luck!" she patted Alira as horse and rider left to prepare to enter the big, flat arenas, which were daunting for Alira, for she would have to work in a big, open space.

Ingrid felt a flutter of nerves as they trotted between the boards, then gave her mare a squeeze to get her going forward. There followed a very acceptable test with no misdemeanours on Alira's part; perhaps it lacked the impulsion and accuracy they normally achieved, but they were very pleased with her.

Waiting for the Novice class, Ingrid went and walked her horse across some of the big fields where people were walking horses, lunging them, riding them, or just letting them graze. Lucy leaned on the fence, feeling the warm sun on her skin, warming her through to her bones and energising her in a way that was rare in the colder north of England. This was ethereal, almost unreal; they were living the dream. Ingrid was hot as she sat on her mare, letting her stretch and getting her to relax; she felt the same glow of happiness as Lucy. This was just what she wanted to do, train her horse, keep improving her, compete and learn, blaze a trail with this magic horse. Alira was enabling two amateurs to experience competitive dressage and have a lot of fun!

Her best achievement over the three days was fifth place in the Novice class, which meant she stood above another thirty horses and wow, was she proud of herself in that prize-giving!

"Like a little saint she was!" Ingrid enthused, as she rode her out of the grass arena where prizes were awarded.

Adorned with her fabulous rosette, long ribbons trailing, Alira seemed to know she was special when she was in there and while other horses played up, ran back, or bucked in the lap of honour, she was her best self.

"Yes," laughed Lucy, "She looks smug, I think she's smiling!"

This was the final day and now they untacked, took her plaits out and left her sporting a frilly mane, while she ate her hay. They got busy loading up the horsebox and noticed that the weather was changing – dark clouds obscured the sun and a distant rumble suggested an approaching storm. All too quickly it was upon them, the heavens opened and rain pelted down. People were rushing everywhere, hurrying horses out of the rain, grabbing belongings before they got wet.

Ingrid and Lucy hurried to Alira's stable, worried that she would be frightened by the noise as rain hammered on the canvas roof; but no, she was calm, even though she was marooned! The stable was quickly filling with water and Alira was standing on an island at the back, unperturbed, just eating hay. Her owners laughed at her unexpected acceptance of the situation, but soon got her out and got her loaded; to sleep again on the way home, as she had the previous year.

Was the thunderstorm a harbinger of doom where their horses were concerned? They travelled back to Normanton safely but did not like what they found when they got there.

Chapter 26
Feeble Deception

Alira was delighted to have time out in the field the day after she got back. James had been looking after Mervyn, who had been turned out by himself while they were away. But that day, the 'Riding School' at Normanton were having a 'Pony Day', where children could come and 'own a pony' for a day, take part in mounted games and ride across the cross-country course.

That evening, Lucy caught Mervyn while Ingrid got Alira from out of the field. Lucy was alerted to an inexplicable mark on Mervyn's back. There was a sweaty mark where a saddle had been! Alira seemed a little awkward in her gait, something about the way she placed her hind legs was unusual.

"Ingrid!" Lucy called sharply. "Someone has been riding Mervyn."

"No!" Ingrid was aghast.

That someone had taken their pony out of the field without their permission was incomprehensible and then to have ridden him too! Ingrid tackled Anita about it, who initially denied that anyone would take him out of the field, but then placed the onus onto her daughter, that she sorted out which ponies did 'Pony Day'; but she was talking to a psychologist. Ingrid could tell she was lying. Anita went on to admit there was a pony that 'looked like Mervyn' involved – Mervyn was fairly unique around there, the only pure white pony, so her denial did not ring true. Taking Mervyn without asking was wrong, as was riding a pony who has suffered a broken leg, which incidentally, the Riding School had been instrumental in causing. The worst injustice lay in him having been taken from the field leaving Alira alone. Ingrid and Lucy could see the evidence of the mare's consequent behaviour – lines of hoof prints up and down the fence, skid marks where she had turned to dash back, because her friend had gone. She had caused damage to her legs in doing this and there were bitter consequences for the horse and her owners.

Chapter 27
A Professional Yard

This outrageous violation of owners' rights at the livery yard was a final straw for Lucy and Ingrid. For too long they had been treated rudely and inconsiderately. They were struggling to help Alira and Mervyn cope with the heat and flies from the muckheap, which now encroached on the whole block of stables, literally outside the windows; there were dangerous amounts of building materials laid around and the new layout represented a significant fire risk. Turning the horses out was not allowed if any kind of event was going on, it had rained or there was maintenance taking place on the cross-country course. The arenas were of considerable advantage to them but now were often in use and liveries had to wait until they were free, on top of that Anita had begun to levy a charge for even the shared use of any arena. The unpleasant atmosphere was noticed by a few of the liveries, who wondered about financial problems, but in Lucy and Ingrid's case they could not help but wonder if jealousy was a factor, for Alira was winning more than any of Anita's family horses.

What could they do about it? Every time they had raised issues they were met with irritation and antagonism, however nicely they tried to negotiate and ultimately any person with a horse at livery does not want to disadvantage their own horse by being seen as a troublemaker. Lucy deliberated about taking legal action after having Mervyn taken out of the field, but the action and its consequences would be hard to prove and would be met with denial for sure. There was only one other option: to leave.

Miranda had offered them a stable for Alira at her dressage yard and said she also had a shed for Mervyn. They thought Miranda's schooling arena was fabulous and it was continuously available, as was an area to turn them out into, so they made the decision, gave notice and left.

Scott Farm where Miranda lived and worked was just down the road and offered livery, including a big stable, a stable for Mervyn, a small, even, flat field for the two of them and two schooling areas. One Saturday before Christmas saw them packing up again, lock, stock and barrel into the horsebox, then a journey to get a supply of hay, followed by the last run, to get the two equines, load them into the trailer and head out. There were no hard feelings, for the new livery stables were run by Miranda's uncle; they promised to come back for lessons when Alira was in training again.

The horses settled quickly into this professional yard and frequently Ingrid could ride in the arena and have it all to herself. Lucy would film her and they would analyse the film together over coffee on the weekend. During one of these sessions, they noticed something on film that they had been unaware of: just a slight toe-drag on the off hind.

Part 3

Chapter 28
Dark Clouds Gather

Their loyal, experienced vet was called and he found a dramatic lameness in the off hind after a flexor test. This is where the vet holds up the hind leg to fully flex all the tendons and ligaments, then immediately has the horse trotted away, revealing any problems in a more obvious way than would otherwise be perceived. He immediately referred Alira to the Browning Equine Hospital for a scan.

Instead of going to their next competition, they were loading the horse into their box for a medical procedure, not anything she would object to, but not what she and her rider really wanted to do. They journeyed towards the Equine Hospital with their horse compliant in the back, Lucy at the wheel and Ingrid alongside, cheerful and oblivious to the events the day would bring, that would begin to change everything.

The mare was excited when they unloaded, thinking that this must be a party! She had one brief fit of panic about a leaf-blower that was being used to keep the place tidy; the premises were, indeed, immaculate. Lucy walked her around, familiarising her with the surroundings, which, unknown to them, would all too soon become very familiar. When they had to lead her down the ramp into the clinic area, she was tall and a little tense. Maybe she was remembering the ceratohyoid operation. This time, all that happened was that a scanning device was passed over her hind leg from hock to hoof, Ingrid avidly discussing what she and the vet could see, as he explained the images on the screen, Lucy holding and reassuring the mare with her voice and touch.

The verdict was that the suspensory ligament in Alira's off hind leg was torn. Ingrid felt darkness descending, a sinking feeling of despair and injustice that this should be the outcome, confirming her worst fears, which she had dismissed as just a nightmare scenario that surely would not happen to them.

Lucy heard a door slam in her head and their dreams were behind that door, inaccessible because of this diagnosis. They both knew that the sport of dressage put strain on the suspensory ligaments and that an injury like this would severely limit her career. Lucy and Ingrid were choked up, devastated by the news that their one and only horse was damaged, their beautiful mare, the horse that they had struggled to develop, but had the potential to be a top-class dressage horse. This could not and must not be. But the evidence was in front of them and the veterinary surgeon was one of the best, he would not be wrong. Why this horse! Why now, when so much was just beginning?

The vet sensed their distress and tried to reassure them that there was treatment, there were possibilities. Lucy looked into the brown eye of her mare so close to her face, so calm and lovely, happy and content; of course, they would treat her, of course they would do everything within their power to put things right.

There was a feeling of unreality within both of them as he carried on talking about solutions. They were in a space somewhere else, that nobody else could understand, his words were echoing down a tunnel and could not quite reach them, even though the meaning was clear. The reality was cruel, let it be a bad dream.

"We can give her shock wave therapy, start today with the first session of it."

There followed a long list of instructions and new appointments and then they took turns to hold Alira while shock therapy took place on her hind leg, from hock to fetlock; both hind legs because they had found slight inflammation in the other leg, a common occurrence because the other leg is taking the strain from the demonstrably lame leg. The treatment was painless and would hopefully provoke the tendons and ligaments to gradually heal.

Three months of rest was prescribed. Exactly how were they going to get her to stay sane without her work? Dressage was the only thing that utilised her fire and energy, channelled it into safe parameters where she could move and express herself harmlessly.

Ingrid was stoic. "We'll just have to do it; she will get better if we do as he says."

The only exercise classed as suitable for Alira was walking on hard ground, so Lucy was well placed to help with that! The mare would need another treatment in two weeks, another after four and it should be concluded with a final treatment after six weeks.

When they arrived back at their stables, it was late and Ingrid had to go. Lucy finished the jobs then stood with Alira, contemplating her mare, who looked back at her, slightly quizzical, sensing the gravity of Lucy's stare. Lucy wondered what it was about that beautiful, gentle face that calmed all conflict, obliterated all bitterness and made sense of life when it was otherwise crazy and inexplicable. Perhaps it was the symmetry, the graceful lines, the delicacy and purity of the sculptured nostrils, the exquisite lines of her ears sweeping forwards, the curve of her rounded cheekbones and that long nose. Most probably it was the deep, dark pools that were her eyes, heavily lashed and darkly defined, mysterious with colours that reflected her coat and with a central cube that gave a promise of intelligence and kindness that was both wholesome and intriguing.

Their bay mare was a treasure – but treasure is fought for, gained and lost, just as each day with a horse can dawn as insipid, become as bright and amazing as the midsummer solstice then cool in the chill of the evening. What would become of Alira when the shadows drew down, pain blurred the edges of sanity and created a new character, less attractive and more dangerous?

The farrier removed her shoes and the presumed remedy commenced. The vet had advised that they should only walk her on hard ground so Ingrid rode her down the drive from Miranda's yard; Alira was still fit and full of herself, not easy to ride at all when all she was allowed to do was walk! Lucy sometimes led Mervyn alongside her and their horse relaxed a little into this new regime, but her demeanour was not helped by the weather beginning to turn wintry as the month wore on. October brought wind, hail and rain. Mervyn's shed, which was where they kept most of their equipment, began to fill with water. The motorway ran adjacent to the arena and the constant traffic precipitated a layer of grime over everything. The task of keeping the shed dry and warm for Mervyn and abating the spiders and cobwebs was laborious. Also, devising a way of preventing Mervyn from eating the hay which they stored in there was a challenge. It was behind a wooden gate but he was not averse to putting his hooves on one of the higher bars to enable him to have a feast that he really did not need!

The time passed and two more treatments took place, then followed rehabilitation; four *more* weeks where trot could be introduced, but still on hard ground, so they could not use the big arena that they had moved to Miranda's establishment for! Great excitement accompanied her first trot for months – she jumped off her hocks and looked level behind! All was looking good. The following month, she was scanned again and this revealed impressive healing and improvement, with very little inflammation left. Their hopes soared and they could do light work on hard ground, walk and trot only, for another month, then very gradually increase her exercise until she could start proper work six months after the original diagnosis.

The winter months were bringing problems; however, there were no lights in Mervyn's stable and all their kit was dirty, dusty and covered in mildew. Not such a good shed, after all. Alira's stable was part of a new build, but outside of the main American barn style of stabling which Miranda used; hence, it was a long way from the water supply. Security at the premises was excellent, but the huge, heavy, locked metal gates presented serious difficulties on cold, dark, wet winter nights, when they had to wrestle with the complex set of locks and keys while the wind tried to whip the gate away from them or break the limb that held onto it. The small paddock provided for turning their horse and pony out had not much grass and Alira had nothing to distract her from antics which she seemed to design to put maximum strain on her hind legs.

The mare did not seem to be thriving either; she had constantly loose stools and a poor appetite. The vet had checked her teeth, she had been wormed, but to no avail, she still seemed listless at times, even though her usual fiery self when being turned out: several girls that worked for Miranda had been knocked for six when they released her into the field!

Chapter 29
Mysterious Malaise

Arriving at Brough Farm, they were greeted by the owners, Laura and Chad, attractive, kind people in their fifties who had diversified their farming into livery stables that utilised the old farm buildings. Alira would be in a building that also housed several interesting partnerships; 'Swearing Sarah' had an ex-racehorse, which had been in her care during her working life as a head girl at a racing yard, and she had kept him after injury ended his racing career. Sarah's conversations were littered with expletives and exaggerations but she was actually very kind and friendly with a wicked sense of humour! Her horse was a beautiful chestnut gelding which she kept in excellent condition.

Two years previously, this yard had a Strangles outbreak, an invasion of a disease which kills many horses. Sarah's horse was a victim but she had nursed him back to health, meanwhile keeping him in strict quarantine.

Pleasant, mild mannered Amy was in the stable next door to her, she had a Welsh Cob mare which she kept indoors a lot because she had sweet itch, a skin irritation that is exacerbated by flies. When Amy rode her, the mare was awkward and stubborn enough to deter Amy from riding again, then when she finally did, the problem was even worse. Eventually, Amy overcame her horse's inhibitions about work and had some great riding on her; it materialised that Amy had been injured previously in a fall from another horse, which had shaken her nerve.

Another young woman had the horse opposite Alira, a sensible grey Irish gelding, a good fun all round horse, whose character was non-threatening to Alira because when not being ridden he was usually asleep! Adjacent to him was an army girl's horse, ex-cavalry so tall and dark, but he was much fatter than he would have been in his army days and consequently naughtier in a mischievous way. Right next to Alira was a big carthorse type of creature, mighty like his owner and he was always being washed; he was clipped and rugged up so hopefully kept warm, although he was frequently wet! The stable on the other side was home to a grey pony belonging to Penny, who also owned a piebald cob in the stable beyond that. She was vivacious and friendly; in fact, everyone was friendly, until they met Lucia, known as Luke.

Introducing herself, Lucy was taken aback when the retort was, "I know who you are and we don't want you here!" With which she stormed off, back into the other barn, which was where Mervyn was going to live, right opposite her horses, of which there were four!

"She thinks you will have brought ringworm with you, because Miranda's horses have got it." They were told later; this latter was purely gossip, Miranda had no horse with ringworm.

Ingrid and Lucy discussed this affront that evening. "I recognise her," said Ingrid and Lucy agreed that she looked familiar.

"Think!" demanded Ingrid. "Remember when we first had Alira? Remember those people that used to sit in the barn smoking, at the Equestrian Centre? She was one of them!"

Suddenly, Lucy recalled, "She was the one who used to whack her horse and never spoke to anybody except that other snooty woman with the dressage horses!"

Four years had passed and here she was, back to cause trouble. They never had stood up for themselves particularly, back then, but decided they would now. The next morning, they confronted her and this time, the livery owner, Chad, got involved, having heard that there was an altercation in his yard. He told Luke that she could either be civilised or she must leave. Strangely, there followed a complete change of heart on Luke's part and she became friendly, anxious to help, would feed Mervyn in the morning for them and asked Ingrid to give her dressage lessons, for which she paid her properly.

They were cautious when they first put Alira out in her new field, although the field seemed ideal there was no telling whether Alira would settle. Obviously, she was accompanied by Mervyn, who was unperturbed by the motorway being next door to it and most interested by the abundant grass. Their mare was excited at first and had a buck and a kick and not too much galloping. She was not as fit now after all her weeks of rest and soon settled to graze. This was an excellent start, for it was imperative that she did not hammer those hind legs too much. With cautious optimism, they turned her out the following day, before going to work. This was Alira Compliquer though, a fact not to be forgotten.

The farm where they now had stabling was again, adjacent to the motorway, across from which was an army camp. Alira was not upset about the motorway, having been habituated to that whilst at Miranda's establishment. But hidden terrors had always haunted Alira and that very first day in the field was interrupted by a freak occurrence; a terrorist alert! Unbelievable. This had never happened at this establishment, and never did again, but it happened on Alira's first day out in her new field.

The motorway was closed, all the noise becoming a puzzling quietness, quickly punctuated by the vibrating throb of helicopters; as if that was not enough, lines of soldiers began combing the fields, looking for people or objects presumably.

The first that Laura knew about it was when a uniformed officer knocked on the farmhouse door to say that there was a horse 'going mad in the field out here'.

Laura went out, caught Alira and brought her in, not knowing of Alira's reputation for wildness. She managed the mare without a problem; perhaps Alira was so frightened that she did actually want to stay by her side! The hoofmarks in the field were testament to her alarm, as was the dried sweat on her flanks that Ingrid saw when she came to do evening stables.

"Oh, that defies belief," Lucy gasped when Ingrid rang to report the day's events.

The odds must have been stacked high, that such an event would ever happen, but it had to be that first day in the field and Ingrid was fraught with worry about the effect of the galloping on her horse's hind legs; Alira's alarm cannot have done them any good.

The two women were ill from digging out and dusting down Mervyn's shed when they left Miranda's and now both of their animals developed a deep, dry cough. The local vet was called, for antibiotics, work had to be light for a few days. Then they got going again and Alira was doing some super work, but inevitably she came in one day with her off hind leg filled. They worked on it with cold-water hosing, applied leg guard and clay.

Soon, the filling subsided and she was working out of her skin, amazingly well behaved, but perhaps she was a little bit off colour they thought. Sure enough, within another couple of days, a lump developed on her cheek and her nose was running. A day after that, she had lumps on both cheeks, her head was swollen so that her bridle barely fitted and she was lethargic and unbalanced to ride. Occasionally, she coughed and choked on her hay and her stools were loose again. The local vet referred her back to the Equine Hospital for a gastroscopy, as he thought something was wrong in her gut.

"Here we go again," said Lucy, as she drove away from Brough Farm with Alira in the horsebox.

Unfortunately, they were not going anywhere to have fun or test themselves against other competitors, just going to the hospital with yet another problem. Upon arriving there, Alira was taken off them by the senior vet who had dealt with her previously, only this time he was surrounded by students, learning from his experience.

"Now this horse is usually gleaming," he told them, "The suggestion that something is wrong is very apparent."

Lucy and Ingrid were suddenly aware just how different their horse looked to how she usually did; yes, she had lost top line and muscle during her long, enforced rest period, but she had always been sleek and shiny. Suddenly, she looked thin, her coat lacked lustre and her whole manner was subdued, where was their wild girl?

Extensive research upon Alira by more than one vet revealed that she had inflammation in her chest and they suspected inflammatory bowel disease. Her stay in hospital lasted longer than they had planned; she was kept in for four days. Her two owners visited her on alternate days, comforting her with grooming, lots of rugs and attention, but she was not allowed any titbits. When at last she came back from the Equine Hospital, she started to get better on a diet rich in oil and protein, very little grass, hay which had been soaked overnight and light exercise. Gradually, her esprit returned, but it was well into spring when she finally started to be more like her old self.

Soon, to their great relief, she was healthy again and they took her to the first Equestrian Centre where she had won classes; she qualified for Trailblazers again, then they took her further afield and she won one class then behaved badly in the next, so badly that she was last! Back home, Lucy was thrilled because Ingrid started practicing some dressage to music, but just prior going back to have her suspensory damage checked, the mare started to feel disunited for Ingrid in canter, then the next time she rode her would not engage her hind legs properly.

Gloom descended upon them, "We seem to have constant worry."

"Sometimes I wonder whether we should just retire her and put her in foal," confided Lucy.

However, the check-up found no inflammation in her hind legs and put the awkward movement down to a bad back, for which she had some physiotherapy. This was expensive, not covered by insurance and they had just received an enormous vet bill from the stay in hospital; Lucy started to pursue this through insurance, but soon the premium became too expensive to afford and they could no longer insure their problem prone mare.

Alira was soon feeling fit again after back therapy and then her latest nonsense was to be frightened of a foal which came to the livery stables! Horrified by this small and impertinent being, she decided the best policy was to bolt, or if restrained from that, rear. Ultimately, she did befriend the foal and was mildly embarrassed when she realised that it was one of her own species. Not so the goats who inhabited a garden near the gatehouse of the farm. They were not her species and had a very strong smell so were intolerable to Alira.

Leading her up the drive to the little house, she would get more and more alarmed, snorting and shaking her head as if to say, "Oh no, goats again, let me go!"

During the evening of one of the first days with clement weather, Lucy was stood talking to the young guy, Graham, who lived at the gatehouse, when Chad came by in his land rover. Alira was stood tall and tense because of the goats, hence looking very beautiful and Chad observed her appreciatively.

"A good advert for the place" he commented.

"Who?" laughed Graham, "This lady or the horse?"

"Well, both, actually," answered Chad, then drove away, embarrassed!

Lucy chuckled to herself, because it was one of the first days where she had not been wearing double layers of coats and jumpers! Without a hat, her hair flowed down her back, her healthy complexion belied her years. She did notice now, though, that it was the older men who looked at her, the younger ones always looked at Ingrid. Then everyone looked at their horse, she bloomed again and was full of dash and danger.

During this spring, her work was okay, but she was often defiant and unwilling to cooperate with her schooling, then when she did, canter transitions caused an issue; she preferred to take a great leap rather than a smooth transition. Ingrid just could not get her back to her pre-suspensory injury performance and was unable to get the same feel from her canter. Was it difficult for her to work from behind? Was she just being reluctant to work, after her long, enforced rest, or was there still some problem, perhaps numbness?

Maybe, Ingrid thought, she was not asking the right questions and she needed some expert guidance. Lucy gave as much input as possible but could not really see the difficulties Ingrid was having. The troubles she could see were indicative of suspensory damage, but she was supposed to be recovered or at least improved. However, she had lost elasticity in her hind legs and the horse simply could not perform as she had been doing previously. Ingrid was reluctant to take her up to Miranda for help, as Alira clearly now preferred much firmer surfaces than the very loose one where Miranda gave her lessons.

Hence there was, one fateful day, a long journey down towards the South of England to have a lesson from a renowned dressage professional, who in his retirement did clinics and lessons for dressage riders. They went full of excitement, convinced that he would love their little horse and impart some gems of wisdom to enhance forever their dressage training.

Nothing could be further from the truth.

Chapter 30
Too Dangerous for Dressage

Ingrid went to see a previous lesson finishing, after they had taken Alira out of the horsebox. Left in charge of the mare, Lucy was struggling to make sense of her; two stallions in an adjoining stable yard were shrieking to her, she was in season and was incredibly excited. Leading her round to calm her down was an anachronism, for it actually seemed to be winding her up. Lucy had to resort to tying her to the waggon whilst she waited for Ingrid, staying by the mare of course, to see she was safe.

Upon Ingrid's return, she got the tack out of the locker, Lucy rubbing Alira down in the sun. Having the saddle on seemed to escalate her excitement and suddenly she swung her quarters around, knocking Lucy, who was standing next to her, off balance and sending her spinning towards the concreted ground. Luckily, Ingrid grabbed her arm to stop her from falling, then finished tacking up with firm words for the mare. A little shaken, Lucy went to watch the lesson and prepared to be impressed, but she was not at all.

The instructor said little, slurring his words and appearing to be impatient with having to teach, with the horse and with Ingrid. A woman of similar age was assisting him and made various less than positive comments about Alira as well as Ingrid's riding. Ingrid was struggling to manage her mare, who uncharacteristically, was fighting for her head and leaping into the air every time Ingrid asked her for collection, transition or change of direction. The instructor and his assistant decided in their wisdom that what she needed was side reins, which they fixed onto her bridle and thence to the saddle, also a so-called check rein, which acted a bit like a standing martingale. They insisted that Ingrid rode with short stirrups, which did not seem right for dressage and seemed to make the mare angry.

Now she cantered away up the long side and when Ingrid tried to turn her onto a circle, leaped, then reared vertically and the unthinkable, the unbearable, happened. She went right over backwards, crashing down towards her rider. Lucy ran to Ingrid who lay crumpled at the side of the fence; Ingrid saw her coming, as if in slow motion, through a quavering sea.

Then there were frantic questions from Lucy. "Are you all right? Don't get up if you hurt anywhere, do you? Are you okay?"

But Ingrid was getting up, the horse's body had missed her, just the knee blocks on the saddle had hit her head and her arm had been gashed on the fence. Later, she realised she was suffering from concussion, but just then she was looking for her horse, who had jumped up and cantered to the top of the arena. Lucy did not care where the horse was, she was so upset, she thought that Alira had landed on Ingrid. Now she was relieved, but still concerned; the two 'experts' saw that Ingrid was on her feet then just went away, saying the horse could not be a dressage horse – it was dangerous.

Their attitude was unbelievably arrogant and dismissive, and the two women were left to sort themselves out. Eventually, Alira had to be caught and re-loaded into the horsebox. Ingrid went and washed the dirt out of the wound on her arm and was unable to find anyone to register any kind of complaint.

Mostly, Ingrid and Lucy just wanted to get out of there; they drove the long journey home, with a compliant and subdued Alira in the back. Inevitably, a lot of questions went through their heads, why had neither of them pointed out that the mare was not happy, that force and subjugation had never worked with her? They were so sure that these people knew more than they did that they had just accepted their ideas, but now thought that these so-called experts really could not deal with a feisty mare like Alira. Maybe these people would only work with placid, obedient horses who did not put up a fight and could be moulded easily into any kind of behaviour.

Maybe, though, there was something wrong with Alira; she was usually sweet and kind in the stable, but work did seem to be bringing out the worst in her just lately. Perhaps she was in pain and because those people had tried to force her into a method of going that was painful to her, she had objected to protect herself? Maybe the stallions had made her excessively hormonal, for indeed her seasons seemed to be getting stronger and more noticeable as she got older. The gloom within the horsebox on the long road home was palpable and the journey seemed never ending.

The days that followed saw Ingrid back in the saddle and the mare doing some lovely work, contradicting the claim that she could not be a dressage horse. One blustery summer's day, they took her to the Equestrian College venue where she had to deal with the proximity of cattle. In the warm-up arena, she was volatile and Ingrid had images of her horse going up and over on top of her again, so gradually the tension was building in them both and Lucy had to come into the arena to get hold of the mare's head. It is not technically allowed to have someone on foot in the warm-up arena, so they took their horse to stand outside the indoor arena.

With Lucy at her head and Ingrid on her back, she stood stock still, pricked ears and flared nostrils detecting noises and smells of cattle, which were right next to the equine area today. And must have previously escaped into the horse box park for there was evidence in the form of cow-pats there when they unloaded her, immediately unsettling her and causing her to be a handful for Lucy as she led her around. Alira responded extremely well to the superb surface in the indoor arena under normal circumstances, so maybe she would improve in there today.

Eventually, their name was called and Lucy went with them to the door, then scooted away to find a seat in the spectator's gallery. Alira and Ingrid trotted in, looking as if they meant business. She tried to shy at the judge's table but Ingrid pushed her on firmly; the bell rang and they entered the white boards, to produce a lovely test, with no misbehaviour whatsoever.

They gained second place in a big class and she came away with a luxurious blue rosette. They felt exonerated by this prize and slightly reassured about their horse; she seemed to be a different and more difficult beast to handle just lately and the spectre of the suspensory damage hung over them. It was anxiety provoking to work her too much but she became harder to handle when she did not get enough work. She looked really well now, but quite often wore her angry mare face, making them wonder whether it was due to her hormones or to discomfort.

Chapter 31
A Warning

The next competition saw her complete and win two affiliated Novice tests, with high scores in big classes. This was quickly followed by their third year of competing at the Trailblazer's Championships, for which they had qualified earlier in the year. Given her recent wins and the fact that on a good day she was actually working at Elementary level, they went with high hopes of this being a successful outing. But when she came out of the horsebox, she was a demon mare that seemed determined to cause havoc. Reliably, when Alira was at her most explosive, various things came to add to her volatility.

While presenting a display of being the most disobedient horse on the showground, a low-flying aircraft sent her into a spin, then somebody decided to put a tent up. People vanishing under canvas and then reappearing again, whilst the canvas flapped in the wind, was a good excuse to snort and shy and whirl Lucy around, making the journey to her stable, instead of a pleasant walk, a gruelling battle to hang onto her and not to be trampled under her feet. Interestingly, there was an entire horse stabled near to her row of boxes, he was calling to her and she was very aware of his presence. Alira was thinking about breeding, not focusing on what her owners wanted her to do! Once in her stable, she seemed reasonably settled and they went to find their accommodation then came back to walk her out and finally, settle her down for the night, without any drama.

Their class was early the next day and the day turned out to be stormy; the rain stopped after an early downpour, then the wind proceeded to pick up, flapping the flags and tents and making horses skittish. Nervously, Ingrid took the little horse into the warm-up arena and tried to find herself a space where she could work quietly and settle her down. Alira was fine until asked to canter, when she did her leaping style of transition to then come down heavily onto Ingrid's hands.

When it was time for her to go over to Lucy to have her boots taken off, Ingrid was not feeling happy about their preparation. "She just feels unreliable, she is not always listening to me and she will not bend when I ask her."

"Remember when you did that test at the college, you did no warm-up at all and she was fine when she got into the arena," Lucy pointed out.

Ingrid said, "I suppose so, but today I have been put in that far arena, we know she doesn't like open spaces and just now she's been reacting to the flags, which she has never done before."

The wind was furiously flapping the flags and some of them snapped against the flagpole making a sound like the sharp crack of a whip.

"Just keep your legs on and coax her, she'll be all right once you start the test," said Lucy, hoping she was right.

But the look in Alira's eye suggested she might not be.

Ingrid rode her carefully down the edge of the other arenas when her turn came, feeling as if her horse's hooves were on springs, but arriving at the far arena without mishap. She was determined now to keep her going forward, focus her on her job so that she did not look at the wide, open space beyond the arena and let panic set in. The bell went and Ingrid perhaps did the fastest test she had ever done, feeling that if she let Alira stop working for a minute she would be off! Back to the safety of her stabling post haste, no doubt. Alira felt on the verge of melt down all the way through, but somehow Ingrid got her to do everything correctly, even to halt and salute the judge, but to 'leave the arena on a long rein' as instructed was never going to happen; as soon as Ingrid fractionally dropped the contact Alira stood up tall on her hind legs.

Ingrid slipped off, hanging grimly onto her horse who now seemed huge, stood up above her – and as soon as she was down was battling to get away. The sheet from the test would point out that, "You should not dismount before leaving the arena" but, the judge continued, "He was a bit excited today."

That was an understatement! Why did judges always misjudge her gender when she was being difficult? Maybe Alira looked more like a stallion than the ones she desperately wanted to be with!

Ingrid was in the arena with both hands on the reins trying to bring her down and take her out. She dreaded to think what would happen if she let go of her. She was like a coiled spring and would do her 'pocket rocket' between the other six arenas, endangering other people's safety or at the very least ruining their tests. Beyond this lay the warm-up arena and mayhem would ensue if she bolted through there, after which there was the danger of her galloping through spectators, which did not bear thinking about. Lucy was watching what was happening and could see the risk of Ingrid losing her, so quickly was racing to help, dodging officials and stewards, grabbing the horse as soon as she got to her and letting an exhausted Ingrid get her breath back. Although before they arrived back at the warm-up area, she too had to get hold at the other side of her bridle, such was Alira's determination to get away as fast as possible. What was she running from? Was it pain? Could she be wanting to get towards something, perhaps her stable or the stallion who had been calling her? Lucy and Ingrid regretted so many times, that horses could not talk.

Ingrid was furious with the mare for such an incoherent display of bad behaviour and had angry words to get her to calm down and walk back to the stable. Amazingly, she did become calmer, walking with exaggerated alacrity, sweating as if she had run the Grand National but losing her manic countenance and finally, tuning in to her owners again, listening to their words, responding to them. Ingrid's fury had shocked her back into reality, but Ingrid did get a warning from a steward for talking to her horse like that! Had they let Alira take flight in the middle of the competition, or even on return to the stables, the consequences would have been such that actually, the steward should have been thanking them!

Their arms ached and they were depressed by this turn of events, possibly a sign of returning suspensory ligament inflammation.

Chapter 32
A Danger to Herself

Back at Brough Farm, she settled into her new livery stables and they worked her in the two arenas. She worked as if it was a different horse that they had with them that day at the Trailblazers Championships.

Then one night, when Ingrid was working her in the big sand arena, she almost had a rotational fall, when her forefoot got caught in a hole. Thankfully, she staggered forwards and her momentum kept her going. Ingrid stayed firmly in her saddle and no harm was done. The school was not forgiving terrain and Ingrid decided to use the smaller arena, with a better surface. Using this, Alira did some of the best work she had ever done and fellow liveries watched in awe, soon they were asking Ingrid to give them lessons and she quite enjoyed trying to improve other people's horses and their way of going – especially when she got paid for it too!

Only a few days after her return from the infamous championships at Stoneleigh, they took her to the Equestrian Centre which was overshadowed by a huge power station, over to the East of the A1, where she had been known to leap a mysterious part of the arena. But today she worked her test to show off all she had got. Ingrid rode quietly, effectively, without interfering with her mare and they triumphed over all the other horses that were there: she came home with two firsts in two Novice Affiliated tests. The next few days saw her very chilled out and calm, until one evening Lucy took her to walk around the sand arena after work; it was a dull evening and Alira was on her toes.

Lucy just had the head collar on and the mare walked beside her, the rope hung loosely but she held it tightly. A couple of times the mare shied but Lucy kept hold of her easily and kept out of her way to then bring her back by her side and walk her on. There were various things that spooked her, some colourful jumps, a blue barrel in the corner, the hens that scratched in the hedgerow, but none were really alarming to the horse; she had seen them all before and was just being excitable.

One side of the arena was adjacent to the motorway, but she was well travelled and had lived by motorways for a while now, so the traffic did not bother her. That is, until a police car came past with its siren blaring, followed by three fire engines, all at speed, all with blue lights flashing and a cacophony of sound assailed their ears. The horse was in a total panic; she swung Lucy round and fought for the freedom to flee, facing her, pounding her hooves and shaking her head. Lucy had a reputation for never ever letting go, but half a tonne of horse was desperately trying to get away. The battle seemed to last for minutes but may have been seconds and then the rope was out of Lucy's hands and Alira was away, flat out round the big arena, rope flying, hooves thundering, round and round again with no pause in her headlong gallop.

Lucy was no longer any good at running, but she ran tonight, to get to the gate of the sand arena; she managed to get it shut before the galloping horse approached it and she veered away because it was shut; so at least she was contained, but she still made the most of the opportunity to let herself go. She really did go, full tilt and gathering speed down the long side every time, sometimes Lucy wondered if this was what she needed, the chance to gallop and use up some adrenaline. Lucy once rang a racing yard that had an all-weather gallop, thinking that a whiz around it might steady her behaviour in the field, but Ingrid was singularly unimpressed by the idea.

"She would just drop onto her forehand and gallop herself into the ground," was her verdict and Lucy guessed she was right. But watching her right now, Alira was no longer afraid, she was just enjoying herself.

Eventually, she slowed and cantered to a small gate in a far corner, where a couple of little ponies had appeared from the adjacent field, anxious to join in the fun.

Ah good, thought Lucy, *I'll catch her there.*

Unfortunately, the rope hanging from the head collar, which miraculously she had not stood on yet, caught in the bars of the gate, Alira, still wired, pulled back, felt it pull and threw herself backwards in panic again, fought until the rope came free and was off again. Lucy knew that this would put too much stress on her hind legs; she was also wishing that the small audience by the main gate had not materialised. She ultimately had reason to be grateful to them, however, for the next time that Alira slowed, she went to that gate and Luke grabbed the rope. Alira had run enough now and was prepared to be held until Lucy came. Mortified that she had let her horse free, Lucy thanked them and took the well-exercised Alira back into the yard, floating beside her with exaggerated steps. Lucy walked her until she had stopped sweating and then finished evening stables.

Alira was fit again and so her field behaviour involved galloping too. She would fling herself away from the gate, gallop, swing on her hocks, to gallop the other way and repeat the performance, often skidding to a halt before she turned, putting all her weight onto her hind legs, or she would do a handbrake turn without slowing, as if trying to put maximum strain on her suspensory ligaments.

Unlike some dressage horses, Alira had never been overworked, in fact for much of her life it had been hard to give her enough work, with livery yard restrictions and her owners' work commitments. But she certainly put some strain on her ligaments when she was galloping, because of her huge stride, athleticism, energy and alacrity.

Chapter 33
Ups and Downs

Suspensory inflammation returned and with it despair and disappointment. They no longer had the dressage prospect that they had hoped for. The Equine Hospital recommended an operation to remove the nerve in the hind legs which caused the horse the pain; however, their own vet did not approve of this. Alira was now lame and not able to perform using her power from behind, she fell on her forehand and avoided utilising her hind legs. Ingrid could do walk work on her back and she and Lucy walked her in hand. She could go out in the field but still was liable to gallop. Alira had to be 'let down', which meant cutting her food down, short keep was minimised to almost nothing.

Next, the vets gave her some steroid injections for the inflammation, after which the poor horse had to have three days box rest, then three days walking in hand, then she could be ridden. She was a celebrity when they came to walk her out. Laura commented that she looked as if she was on springs, her action was so elevated and she was so excited. These injections had clearly helped and so when Ingrid rode her again she asked for some work from behind and got it.

Shortly after this, Ingrid briefly went abroad because her partner was working in Europe. Lucy had an experience with Alira that could have been a cataclysmic disaster. Letting her free in the field, the mare bolted and went through all the electric fences, which had made the big field into smaller paddocks. A post then caught on the rope, which was attached to her head collar, and the whole lot went after her: tape and posts, all of it. Alira was galloping around the field dragging this big mess behind her, terrifying herself and in danger of death by a thousand cuts.

When she was exhausted, she let Lucy go up to her and unclip the rope from her head collar, only to shoot away again and continue galloping, while Lucy frantically dragged the mess of tape and poles into the middle of the field so that the horse would avoid them as she flew around. Mervyn was blissfully oblivious to all that was happening, staying near the gate with an expression of 'There she goes again' on his face. Lucy thought she must have high blood pressure now, her heart still pounding long after, while she sorted out the poles, laid them neatly under the hedge, wound up the tape and vowed never again to use electric fencing.

Alira was grazing now, near Mervyn. When Lucy went back to check her, she was in the same place – by the gate – after all that! The whole field was available but she just grazed by the gate all day. Later, when Lucy caught her, she checked every inch of her and found her to be unscathed. Dragging all that fencing on her head collar and galloping like she did would have put strain somewhere, but at least she was resting that week anyway.

When Ingrid came back she was horrified when she heard what had happened, realising that it could have been so much worse. "Mum, you could have been tangled up in all that! It's a good thing you moved quickly and saved the day!"

But Lucy thought she was to blame for further risk to Alira's legs and sanity. Thereafter, when she did morning stables she got James to come with her to turn Alira out into the field, Lucy would bring Mervyn and do the gate while James tried to stop Alira from bolting away. James could hold her longer than Lucy could, but the excited horse still left as if she was coming out of a starting gate as soon as the rope was unclipped from her head collar.

Ingrid was now taking Alira to a local riding school that had an indoor arena with a particularly good surface. A short journey in the horsebox and she was there. Alira worked well on the firm surface, which appeared to be made mostly of sand with a little rubber. The field behaviour continued to be crazy. A fortnight after the fencing incident, Alira escaped from James before she actually went into the field, bolting away up the grassy lane between fields then returning just as fast when she saw Mervyn going up their field, galloped in after him and Lucy slammed the gate. Alira was sweating and shaking, clearly anxious, seemingly more so because she had the whole field available to her; more space did not make her happy, just gave her more anxiety. Plus, she was getting too much good grass, so the electric fence divisions had to be reinstated, although this time the tapes were carefully cut after each smaller field was created, so that the tape was not all joined.

They started to give Alira a calmer prescribed by the vet. They had long since discovered that most of the others available as feed supplements made no difference to her excitability. This one seemed really to help her in the field and when schooling, she became more compliant and seemed to concentrate more easily.

Lucy watched her one day and confirmed to Ingrid that she was going well. "She looks sound and I can see she is light on the hand, coming through from behind and when you were moving her around the school I can see that she is supple."

Ingrid flushed with pleasure and replied that Alira was still full of alacrity, "But I worry all the time that I will ask too much of her and that will inflame her ligaments."

Lucy replied cautiously, "We know the effect of these injections won't last forever, but while she can still do this she should. She loves her work, you can see that."

Indeed, their mare had always been delighted to see her tack come into the stable and she would lower her head for the bridle, open her mouth for the bit and never, ever moved away from having the saddle put on her back.

The New Year was massively wet, the weather mild. Alira was fit and fantastic, Ingrid was working her twice weekly at the local indoor arena because the outdoor schools at Brough Farm were waterlogged. Between these times, Alira was having lots of walking in hand and a couple of hours in the field intermittently. She was good, lightweight and held a deep shine; it was hard to believe that there could be anything wrong. However, she did seem to react to the grass in the field with gastric discomfort, so had to have powders in her feed.

One day, she came in with a strike injury, which enforced some rest and it was clear when Ingrid got back on her that the effect of the steroid injections had worn off, because she felt unlevelled, was toe dragging and refusing to come through from behind.

Later that spring, the injections were repeated. The Equine Hospital vet was prepared to repeat the treatment once more; so, they were on borrowed time.

Chapter 34
How Much Longer?

After the injections, once again, it was three days box rest, then three days walking in hand upon hard ground, then back to normal work. Three days on and Alira has to come out for a walk; any fit horse would play up after three days in the stable and she certainly did. Proud to let her show herself off, Ingrid or Lucy would walk beside her, calm unless she tried to come across in front of them, for this could mean she had the ability to pull away with her weight. Then they would be strict and just hold the whip in front of her chest, firmly commanding her to "walk quietly now, girl" and walked her on smartly, strong hands on the reins. Three more days and Ingrid rode her, declaring her to be fully sound but just too excited to concentrate! Soon she was working brilliantly, at Elementary level too, but only when she had settled down; she was constantly wired and difficult, explosive and strong.

They took her to work at a competition, just to gauge her behaviour, not entering in to any classes. Ingrid did not feel she had control. Alira was so excitable and difficult that they soon took her home, feeling dejected and frustrated. Why was she being so difficult? Alira was eight years old, in her prime but also being a mare through and through; she was moody, unpredictable and when in season quite wild. She escaped from Ingrid the next day, when she was turning her out, galloped down the track, turned around at the end and was coming back just as fast. Ingrid had shut the gate into the yard but saw Alira was coming back at a headlong gallop and wondered how she was going to stop without crashing into the gate. Shouts of "Whoa!" were to no avail, but the mare did not crash into it, instead turning on her haunches at the last minute, pitting all her weight and speed against the very ligaments they struggled to protect.

Three months later, they had the last of the course of three injections and went through the routine again, of three days' box rest, three days walking in hand on concrete and then Ingrid had to be brave enough to get on her back again. She was indeed brave enough and she did handle her horse well under saddle, convinced that at this present moment she was sound again.

Predictably, Alira immediately did something to undermine this. Having never been cast in her life, she got cast in her stable and being Alira, got into a terrible panic. Both Lucy and Ingrid were there, but the horse was stuck at the back of the stable, upside down, hooves flailing, scoring marks in the stonewall as she kicked and writhed, trying to right herself. They could not get near her at first, only try and placate her with soothing calls of "Whoa, girl, whoa, lass" and watch as she kicked hell out of the stone wall with her back legs.

The minute she paused, Lucy dived in and got a rope around her neck, proceeding to try and pull her up with Ingrid's help and using all their might. This was at first ineffective, but as the rope pulled tight it was restricting her breathing and the mare began to get exhausted and became still. Now they could assist her to get up and suddenly she was up, shaking herself off but then standing, head down, clearly somewhat traumatised. Like Ingrid and Lucy.

"Oh, whatever next!" said Lucy.

"I can see her needing some physiotherapy after this," responded Ingrid and they proceeded to brush her down, put in extra shavings to build up her bed even higher at the sides, rugged her up and cautiously left her, slightly shaken by this latest drama.

Inevitably, their horse was stiff next time Ingrid rode. Apart from that, she had numbness in her hind legs and it was as if she needed to learn to use them again. She needed to work, but how much was too much they did not know and sometimes she had to be lunged before Ingrid got on, she was so crazy. These times were worse if she was in season; ultimately, they used a preparation from their vet which helped to reduce the intensity of her seasons but cost a fortune. Lucy and Ingrid had long discussions about Alira having a foal; being at livery stables would make the undertaking challenging and then it would be very expensive too. Whether it was ethical to breed from her was also arguable and for now, this option was discarded. After all, they had heard about the operation which could help her not to feel the pain from suspensory inflammation.

The final injection did not produce any significant improvement and so they made the decision to operate. This was very expensive for them, as they could not claim on insurance anymore. It was not guaranteed to work and involved a very long period of rest and recuperation. They wondered whether they would ever get the horse back, which they had been so successful with, the one that was such a pleasure to work with.

Maybe it was clutching at straws, but maybe this operation would make her comfortable, maybe then she would be less mad. What else could they do? Alira was never going to become a quiet hack for anybody, nobody else could manage her and the option of just turning her away in a field was not feasible, her digestive system could not cope with living on grass and she had so much anxiety in the field.

Chapter 35
Poor Alira

Autumn brought a continuation of the mild, wet weather, but introduced changeability between wild windy days and quiet rainy days, when Alira's hooves splashed through puddles as they walked and walked her. The windy days made her nervous and prone to shy. Chad was desperate to harvest his crops and the grain dryer made a continuous background hum, while tractors sped in and out of the yard, machinery rattling behind. Not conducive to a quiet walk! Alira was quieter than she was, her food was reduced, riding no longer possible, and she had begun to accept that she had this limited life.

The day of the operation drew near and if dark clouds had gathered above Alira, Lucy and Ingrid when they were given the diagnosis of suspensory damage, now it seemed like endless night. Lucy and Ingrid agonised over their decision, to inflict yet another medical procedure on their horse; Ingrid would have prayed if she had been religious and Lucy did because she was.

Alira was in the veterinary hospital for three days after she had the fasciotomy and neurectomy in both hind legs. They visited her every day and the mare seemed uneasy and confused. She had come out of sedation but was still being given a lot of painkiller. Lucy wanted to ride her away into the sunset and never take her to another hospital, but that was not possible and it was going to take all of her and Ingrid's spare time to nurse her back to health – and then what? Ingrid just wanted to be able to ride her and keep her happy and healthy, even if she could not compete.

They brought her home and she went into her stable, clearly happy to be in a familiar environment, promptly having a luxurious roll in her shavings. She kicked all her bandages off whilst doing so and the vet had to be called to reapply them.

Ingrid watched closely to see what to do, wishing she had been a vet instead of a psychologist. The vet welcomed her close attention, dazzled by her lovely smile. Two soft bandages were applied over the dressings, then a whole roll of cotton wool, then elastic bandages, followed by a bigger bandage, on each leg. This procedure was followed for nine days and they never came off when Ingrid had applied them. When they were removed, the legs looked horribly sore from the dressings; many days passed where Alira's owners were very carefully and gently cleaning her legs, while Alira stood patiently, responding to the words 'poorly leg' said in lowered, serious tones.

With such meticulous care, the cuts healed very well and the next stages of recovery stretched before them. She was to be walked in hand on hard ground for five minutes a day for the first week, then ten minutes the next week, then fifteen, then twenty, then half an hour, until after six weeks she was being walked for an hour. There was no horse-walker available to them, so the two of them walked and walked, miles and miles and hours of time, that bay mare beside them and inside them the belief that she would get better, she would be sound and happy. Laura marvelled at their determination and patience as they followed the veterinary instructions to the letter, whatever the weather and no matter if their horse was leaping about; sometimes it took two of them to hold her, one at either side of her, Ingrid holding the reins and Lucy with the lunge rein running through the bit rings. Much of the time, Alira was calm, alert and interested but they could not expect her not to be volatile sometimes, when she was stabled all the time.

The next stage was lunging which gave her a chance to buck and kick, although they tried to keep her mostly in walk and trot. She was moving quite well at this stage, although stiff in her hind legs. Ingrid was watching Lucy one evening when she raised the issue of recovery.

"When I start riding her again we are going to need a firm surface to work on, to give those ligaments the best chance of being okay again."

"Yeah, we'll have to discuss that," was Lucy's hesitant reply. She knew what Ingrid was thinking – that they needed to move again, perhaps back to where they started, the military Saddle Club, where there was an indoor school with a firm surface. Admittedly, the turnout was limited, but it would be fine for Mervyn and Alira could not go out at the moment anyway.

Amazingly, they had discovered that Alira's digestive system was healthier now that she did not graze, which contradicts the common belief that horses need grass and time outside to be healthy. Her enforced box rest had made it difficult to keep her content and well fed, but she was satisfied with two feeds of chaff a day, plus additives and lots of soaked hay; soaked to take out some of the protein and to reduce the dust which might affect her respiratory system.

Chapter 36
Back to Where It All Began

The winter was before them and as the nights drew in, they made the decision and moved their horse and pony to the Saddle Club, back to where they started, but this time they had a bigger, lighter, airy stable. Laura and Chad were disappointed to see them go, but Lucy and Ingrid were single-minded in prioritising what their horse needed; they had invested so much in her, they needed to make sure she recovered from this operation and could work again, comfortably. Alira could do nothing else; she was a liability out hacking and dressage was what she loved when she was in training and her mind could focus.

They had not reached that point yet. Her first ridden work could take place before Christmas and Ingrid bravely mounted, managing to keep her calm in walk, but finding her very tense in the trot. Steady progress was maintained until just before Christmas, disaster struck! She went lame in her near fore and, where the suspensory damage had just limited her movement, now she was dog lame. She could not put weight on that leg. They hosed, they massaged with embrocation, they gave her painkillers, to no avail.

The New Year dawned with dark, wet and windy days, but that made no difference to them: their horse could go nowhere and do nothing. Gloom descended and was hard to shift, inevitably there had to be more days of box rest. She came sound again after a couple of weeks, but the horse, Lucy and Ingrid were losing direction and beginning to doubt what Alira could do and could not do. Ingrid schooled her in the indoor school and made good progress, alternating ridden work with lunge work, but then a fit of bucking on the lunge resulted in the near fore lameness making itself apparent again; she was very lame on that leg.

Alira was crabby and seemed to change the habits of her lifetime, hardly moving in her stable and even lying down during the day. They called the vet; she showed a flash of her old self during trot-up, barging away up the yard, pushing Ingrid to one side, but he could see that something was wrong. Lucy thought that the problem might lie in her horse's shoulder, but that was not the case, the vet thought it could be gravel in her foot. When he had blocked the nerves below her fetlock, she was not lame, so that narrowed down the diagnosis.

There followed more painstaking treatment; the hoof had to be covered by a poultice to draw out any toxin within. This involved trying to get her to keep her foot in a tub of warm water, then drying it, applying a poultice, carefully bandaging that in place then securing it with duct tape repeating the procedure every day, always hoping that there would be something on the dressing to show that poison had come out of her foot, if indeed there was any. They were administering antibiotics for ten days, giving her painkillers that made her food unpalatable and still trying to walk her out in hand; she was strangely subdued and looked dull in her coat. Where had their Alira gone?

Stable duties became a grind, twenty minutes a day walking was hard, she could not go into the indoor school because of the surface getting into the dressing, so most days they walked around the concrete yard in the dark. Most of the liveries had gone home by the time they finished. Lucy would sing the twelve days of Christmas to her horse and the mare would be walking long and low, one ear turned towards her, a resigned acceptance that she yet again had another 'poorly leg' even before the other legs were better.

Due to there being no improvement, the vet came with his X-ray machine and discovered that she had Navicular Disease in that near fore; a crucial bone in the hoof was beginning to degenerate. There could not have been worse news in terms of Alira's future. Ingrid's dread was palpable. Lucy's shock left her speechless, for now, they had a horse who had limitations on three of her legs, one of which had a probably incurable lameness.

The disease – or syndrome as it is sometimes called – is incurable and if they had been going to breed from her it was now impossible, for navicular is a genetic, hereditary issue.

When dreams crash into the dust, they make no sound. For Ingrid and Lucy their life was fractionated in slow motion; there was still hope surely? Hope had become almost ethereal, illusive, wreathing through falling dreams, being now dragged down by difficulty and despair. Hope was made vacuous by tiredness and tears; hope had marched out, leaving only the facts, the undeniable reality which was unthinkable for them right now; but ultimately had to be acted upon and afterwards cannot be denied, for the aftermath is loss.

Remedial shoeing seemed to ease the lameness temporarily but she had to learn to balance herself on some graduated bar shoes, which made her gait uneven. She had become a liability to ride. Ingrid's seat was deep and secure, but Alira's unpredictable behaviour meant she could only be ridden when they had the indoor school to themselves.

One day, she had such an outburst of bucking that she unseated Ingrid, the mare bounced and bounced until Ingrid was dislodged, then got her head down between her legs and twisted in the next leap so that Ingrid went over her horse's shoulder, ripping the skin off the inside of her thigh as she went.

The mare was suffering pain, she was a wild horse, but not a wicked horse, she must have had a reason for so violently ejecting her rider, the rider who had such a harmonious partnership with her in the past. Now they knew the reason and wondered how long this discomfort had stalked their poor horse, making her have these outbursts and not allowing her to recover from the difficulties in her hind legs, exacerbating the problems she had working under saddle.

That was not all. The lying down in the stable, the reluctance to move about in there, then the lameness that was overt, were destroying the horse's will, her very essence was to move, to show herself off, to do dressage. She would never be able to do it now.

Lucy, being Ingrid's mother, usually took the role of reassuring her, comforting her, but now, after the vet had gone, she said, "I cannot bear it, this cannot be happening."

Ingrid said, "I feared it, I dreaded it, but I suspected it. We cannot put this right."

Through tears, Lucy replied, "Everything that has happened to her, every illness, every accident, we have made it right for her, we have got her better, we've overcome the problems one way or another, but now this…"

Ingrid wiped her eyes and looked away. "It's not fair, she is our only horse. How could this happen to us? We were so close to crashing through the barriers we had met, she was right on the verge of being a super dressage horse, moving up the levels, winning a Regional final – and now…"

Neither of them could say more, just hug and turn away to hide their tears, each of them trying to be brave for the other. They gave her a huge bed and a carrot, went home despairing, only to reappear in the morning and walk her out, make her comfortable, not speaking the unspeakable, unable to think, forwards or backwards. They had to go to work and so they did, putting a brave face on it, trying to keep their trouble in proportion, it's only a horse, after all.

There followed another five days box rest, there followed walking out in hand, mile after mile they must have walked, glimmers of hope when she trotted sound on the lunge, only to explode into bucking, galloping and drop back to a lame trot.

Under saddle, Ingrid felt the insecurity of her, the awkward paces and the unwillingness of a horse who had been all about willing and forwardness, the desire to move. Then one day, as soon as Ingrid asked for trot, another eruption of bucking, again dislodging even Ingrid's secure seat, she was hanging on but the bucking did not stop. Alira put a mighty leap in, coupled with a swerve and finally Ingrid went down. Her thigh, already injured, was covered in blood again where the knee block had caught her, a rip that resulted in a scar that lasted the rest of her life.

The deeper scar was the knowledge that her horse did not want to be ridden or schooled, that pain had made her into an unreliable horse who did not want to use herself the way she used to, who actually was becoming a sad and bitter mare whose life was constantly curtailed and a dullness appeared in her eye. Her coat was dull and even as spring had sprung, she did not respond to the joy of longer days.

The pain caused her to stand still in her stable. All the muck was in one pile, she did not want to roll in case she put weight on her near fore as she got up. She would sit like a dog agonising over the best way to jump up, still nervous about her hind legs, up eventually then stood with her head down, unable to understand why her people, who had always made her comfortable, were not doing so now.

Chapter 37
The End

The day dawned cool and with an icy drizzle, the scudding clouds gathering in the West like harbingers of doom and as Lucy drove to the yard a sparrow hawk swooped and took a blackbird, shocking her out of her gloomy thoughts, amazing her with nature's ability to embolden creatures when they are feeding young. Daffodils had bloomed but brought her no pleasure and when she met Ingrid, she could see her calm, composed and beautiful face was like a mask, holding back the tears, circumstances forcing her to put a knife through her own heart. Lucy had arranged it all, but it was Ingrid who led her mare into their horsebox and reassured her that everything was normal, it was just another journey. They drove to the equine hospital in silence. The only sound was the swish of the wipers on the windscreen and an occasional stamp from the mare in the back. Arriving at their destination, to their relief, all was quiet as they led her into a stable. The vet came and explained again that she would simply have an injection, lie down quietly and be gone.

Neither woman could speak and he walked away, leaving them to say their goodbyes. Lucy embraced Alira, her strong brown neck warm and solid, Lucy thought her chest would burst and she left with tears overflowing, thinking she would never be able to stop crying. She wanted to howl but would not upset the horse. Ingrid too was unable to control the tears any longer, she and her mum embraced, hugging hard, finding it almost unbearable to walk away.

They walked past the office, knowing there would be a huge bill to pay but leaving that for another day. For now, it was all over; all the love and the heartache, the joy, fear, disappointment and the other million emotions they had experienced with their wonderful, quirky, amazing horse.

Alira felt no pain, was not alarmed and soon, she went to sleep, then to sleep forever.

They felt as if they could not bear it; they felt so profoundly sad.

Lucy drove away and then pulled the horsebox into the large car park of a garden centre. She looked at her daughter. Ingrid's blue eyes were full of tears. Her big eyes were always expressive and now she looked away to hide her strength of feeling, dropped dark lashes and went pale beneath her natural tan, two pink cheeks showing the fight she was having to hold back her emotion. Her long, tawny hair was piled up on her head and bound by an elegant, narrow plait which looked very sophisticated but Lucy now was remembering the vulnerable child, remembering the day her pony had to go; after she had said goodbye to him with many treats, she had gone to school anyway, to be braver among her friends. Lucy's heart ached, for the loss of their horse, but also with compassion for her daughter, her dreams fallen in the dust.

They went for coffee to delay the return to the yard where they would face the questions, the shock and horror of colleagues who knew that they had faced the most dreaded outcome for any horse owner. They walked like automatons into the café at the garden centre, Lucy sombre, dressed all in brown, but her mood was darker than that. Would they ever be able to move on from here? No horse could ever replace Alira and right then they both felt they would never have another horse.

They knew they had been incredibly privileged to have a horse like her and they knew that if they had another they would know more, be better able to cope with the vagaries of livery yard owners, the moodiness of a mare and the quirkiness of young horses, especially having brought on a high spirited, highly bred Oldenburg. Life would go on, but would never be the same for them, the loss of a beautiful possession, who was a friend, such a character. Alira was an extension of themselves, embodying all that was exciting, courageous, flamboyant, confident and desirable about horses. Nothing could mitigate the pain and sorrow, but the consolation was their memories, the story; the story here told.

Both of them were exhausted after months of nursing a lame horse for whom the veterinary advice was not to let her move and yet their horse was all about movement. They were not as privileged as someone who has their own property and place to keep a horse, thus avoiding the insouciance of the disenfranchised horse owner who pays for accommodation for their equine friends but has no say on the conditions which come with utilising what is often unwanted property. The joy and highlights, defeats and despair, had all been exacerbated by not having the power to make small changes for the good of their horse, a particularly unique individual. One who verged on being crazy, a creature who inspired mixed emotions amongst those who did not own her, not least of these was jealousy.

The empty horsebox, an empty stable, empty hearts for both of them. They had said goodbye forever to Alira Compliquer and the realisation she had gone forever was almost unbearable. Impossible to believe that the great bay solidity of her would not be there in the morning, that never again would they hear her shrill call or the deep rumble of her welcome.

She had changed their life, taken over their life with her needs, the challenges, the fun, the success, exhilaration and disappointments. They had reorganised the rest of their lives to enable them to keep her well and happy, they had enjoyed every minute of having her, until the end, the last year of losing the Alira which they knew and struggling to help her to recover and into the work she loved, failing to resolve that one last irrevocable issue.

The demise of all horse owners is when they lose their animal and for Lucy and Ingrid it was impossible that any other horse would ever replace Alira Compliquer.

CPSIA information can be obtained
at www.ICGtesting.com
Printed in the USA
BVHW061109010719
552382BV00013B/1035/P